DENISE LE

POEMS 19

Books by Denise Levertov

Poetry
Collected Earlier Poems 1940–1960
Poems 1960–1967
Oblique Prayers
Poems 1968–1972
Breathing the Water
A Door in the Hive
Evening Train
Sands of the Well
The Life Around Us
The Stream and the Sapphire
This Great Unknowing: Last Poems
Poems 1972–1982

Prose
New & Selected Essays
Tesserae: Memories & Suppositions
The Letters of Denise Levertov & William Carlos Williams

Translations
Guillevic/Selected Poems
Joubert/Black Iris (Copper Canyon Press)

DENISE LEVERTOV
POEMS 1972–1982

A New Directions Book

Grateful acknowledgment is made to the editors and publishers of magazines and anthologies in which some of the poems in this collection originally appeared: *Alliance for Survival, American Poetry Review, American Report, Anglican Theological Review, The Archive,The Ark, Atropos* (Quebec), *Beloit Poetry Journal, Boston University Journal, Boundary 2, Chicago Review, Clifton, Cold Mountain Press, College of Wooster Yearbook, Confrontation, Copper Canyon, Dartmouth Medical School Journal, Field, The Hampden-Sydney Poetry Review, Hanging Loose, Harper's Magazine, Harvard Magazine, Hearse, I Pass Behind Your Mirror, Images, Imprint, In Our Own Words, In These Times, Intrepid* (Bill Williams and Flossie Special), *Jam To-day, Jawbone Press, Lakes and Prairies, The Lamp in the Spine, Lemming, Liberation, Lost Glove, Mad Dog* (Wales), *Madrona, Moons and Lion Tailes, Mother Jones, Mundus Artium, Nantucket Review, New Directions in Prose & Poetry 29, New Letters, 100 Flowers, Ontario Review, Paintbrush, Paris Review, Peak Load Newsletter, Pearl* (Denmark), *Phoebe, Poetry East, The Poetry Miscellany, Polis Magazine, San Marcos Review, Seer, The Shore Review, Southern Poetry Review, Southern Review* (Australia), *Stuffed Crocodile, Squeezebox, Tendril, Texas Arts Journal, Two Pears Press, West End, Wild Places, Willow Springs Magazine, WIN Magazine, WIP.*

"The Distance" first appeared in *Poetry*. "Chekhov on the West Heath" was first published in a limited edition by Woolmer & Brotherston, Ltd., Gladstone Hollow, Andes, New York. The section "Modulations for Solo Voice" also first appeared as a limited edition, brought out by Five Trees Press of San Francisco, California. "Mass for the Day of St. Thomas Didymus" first appeared in a limited edition from William B. Ewert, Publisher; "Talking in the Dark" was originally published as a Square Zero Editions broadside. The sequence *Pig Dreams* was first published in 1981 in a separate edition by Countryman Press with illustrations by Libe Coolidge.

Manufactured in the United States of America
New Directions Books are printed on acid-free paper.
First published as New Directions Paperbook 913 in 2001
Published simultaneously in Canada by Penguin Books Canada Limited

Library of Congress Cataloging-in-Publication Data

Levertov, Denise, 1923–1997
    [Poems. Selections]
    Poems 1972–1982 / Denise Levertov
    p. cm. – (New Directions paperbook ; 913)
    Contents: Candles in Babylon – The freeing of the dust –
    Life in the forest.
    ISBN 0-8112-1469-9 (acid-free paper)
    I. Title.
PS3562.E8876 A6 2001
811'.54—dc21   00-066424

New Directions Books are published for James Laughlin
by New Directions Publishing Corporation
80 Eighth Avenue, New York 10011

Contents

THE FREEING OF THE DUST (1975)

ONE

From a Plane

Green water of lagoons,
brown water of a great river
sunning its muscles along intelligent
rectangular swathes of
other brown, other green,
alluvial silvers.
                    Always air
looked down through, gives
a reclamation of order, re-
visioning solace: the great body
not torn apart, though raked and raked
by our claws—

Bus

The turnpike, without history, a function
of history, grossly
cut through the woods,

secondgrowth woods without memory,
crowded saplings, bushes entangled,
sparse weedcrop on burned-over sandy embankments.

Brutally realized intentions speed us
from city to city—a driver's world:
and what is a driver? Driven? Obsessed?
These thickarmed men
seem at rest, assured, their world
a world of will and function.

3

Majestic insects buzz through the sky
bearing us pompously from love to love,
grief to grief,
         expensively,
motes in the gaze of that unblinking eye.

Our threads of life are sewn into dark cloth,
a sleeve that hangs down over
a sinister wrist. All of us.
It must be Time whose pale fingers
dangle beneath the hem . . .

Solemn filaments, our journeyings
wind through the overcast.

Knowing the Unknown

Our trouble
is only the trouble anyone,
all of us, thrust from the ancient
holding-patterns, down toward
runways newbuilt,
knows; the strain
of flying wing by wing, not knowing
ever if both of us will land: the planet
under the clouds–
does it want us? Shall we be welcome,
we of air, of metallic
bitter rainbows,
of aching wings? Can we dissolve
like coins of hail,
touching down,
         down to the dense, preoccupied,
skeptical green world, that does not know us?

TWO

In Summer

Night lies down
in the field when the moon
leaves. Head in clover,
held still.

It is brief,
this time of darkness,
hands of night
loosefisted, long hair
outspread.

Sooner than one would dream,
the first bird
wakes with a sobbing cry. Whitely

dew begins to drift
cloudily.
Leafily naked, forms of the world
are revealed,
all asleep. Colors

come slowly
up from behind the hilltop,
looking for forms to fill for the day,
dwellings.
Night
must rise and
move on, stiff and
not yet awake.

'Can't get that tune
out of my head,'

can't get that tree
out of

some place in me.
And don't want to:

the way it
lifts up its arms,
opens them, and–

patient the way an
elderly horse is patient–
crosses them, aloft,

to curve and recross:

the standing, the being
rooted, the look
as of longing.
At each divide,
the choice endured, branches
taking their roads in air.

Glance up
from the kitchen window;
that tree word,
still being said,
over the stone wall.

Fall mornings, its head of twigs
vaguely lifted,
a few apples
yellow in silver fog.

i

Dark, rainsoaked
oaklimbs

within thorny
auburn haze
of brush at wood's edge.

Secretly
I love you, whom
they think I have abjured.

ii

Secretly,
blueveiled
moody
autumn auburn,

you are the very wood I knew
always, that grew up
so tall, to hold at bay

the worldly princes,
baffled and torn
upon the thorns
of your redberried thickets,
may and rose.

Each day
the cardinals call and call in the rain,
each cadence scarlet
among leafless buckeye,

and passionately
the redbuds, that can't wait
like other blossoms, to flower
from fingertip twigs,
break forth

as Eve from Adam's
cage of ribs,
straight from amazed treetrunks.

Lumps of snow
are melting in tulip-cups.

THREE

A Time Past

The old wooden steps to the front door
where I was sitting that fall morning
when you came downstairs, just awake,
and my joy at sight of you (emerging
into golden day–
                the dew almost frost)
pulled me to my feet to tell you
how much I loved you:

those wooden steps
are gone now, decayed,
replaced with granite,
hard, gray, and handsome.
The old steps live
only in me:
my feet and thighs
remember them, and my hands
still feel their splinters.

Everything else about and around that house
brings memories of others–of marriage,
of my son. And the steps do too: I recall
sitting there with my friend and her little son who died,
or was it the second one who lives and thrives?
And sitting there 'in my life,' often, alone or with my husband.
Yet that one instant,
your cheerful, unafraid, youthful, 'I love you too,'
the quiet broken by no bird, no cricket, gold leaves
spinning in silence down without
any breeze to blow them,
                      is what twines itself
in my head and body across those slabs of wood
that were warm, ancient, and now
wait somewhere to be burnt.

All one winter, in every crowded hall,
at every march and rally,
first thing I'd look for was your curly head.

One night last summer in a crowded room
across the ocean,
my heart missed a beat–it seemed I saw you
in the far corner.

You who were so many thousand miles away.

Face

When love, exaltation, the holy awe
of Poetry entering your doors and lifting you
on one finger as if you were a feather
fallen from its wings, grasp you, then your face
is luminous. I saw the angel
of Jacob once, alabaster, stone and not stone,
incandescent.
                    That look, the same,
illumines you, then.
                              But when
hatred and a desire of vengeance
makes you sullen, your eyes grow smaller,
your mouth turns sour, a heaviness
pulls the flesh of your poet's face
down, makes it a mask
of denial. I remember:
from the same block of stone Jacob was carved,
but he was thick, opaque. The sculptor showed
Jacob still unwounded, locked into combat, unblest,

the day
not yet dawning.

What She Could Not Tell Him

I wanted
to know all the bones of your spine, all
the pores of your skin,
tendrils of body hair.
To let
all of my skin, my hands,
ankles, shoulders, breasts,
even my shadow,
be forever imprinted
with whatever of you
is forever unknown to me.
To cradle your sleep.

Ways of Conquest

You invaded my country by accident,
not knowing you had crossed the border.
Vines that grew there touched you.
                    You ran past them,
shaking raindrops off the leaves–you or the wind.
It was toward the hills you ran,
inland–

I invaded your country with all my
'passionate intensity,'
pontoons and parachutes of my blindness.
But living now in the suburbs of the capital

incognito,
       my will to take the heart of the city
       has dwindled. I love
its unsuspecting life,
its adolescents who come to tell me their dreams in the dusty park
among the rocks and benches,
I the stranger who will listen.
I love
the wild herons who return each year to the marshy outskirts.
What I invaded has
invaded me.

FOUR

Photo Torn from The Times

A story one might read and not know
                    (not have to know)
the power of the face–

> 'Ten-year-old Eric
> was killed during racial tension last summer'

> Testimony . . .
> 'tears . . .
> in her eyes . . .
> *"I am not afraid*
> *of anyone.*
> *Nothing else*
> *can happen to me*
> *now that my son*
> *is dead."* '

But the power is there to see, the face
of an extreme beauty, contours
of dark skin luminous
as if candles shone unflickering
on beveled oiled wood.

Her name, Alluvita,
compound of earth, river, life.

She is gazing
way beyond questioners.

Her tears
shine and don't fall.

i   America the Bountiful

After the welfare hotel
crumbled suddenly (after repeated warnings)
into the street,

Seventh Day Adventists brought supplies
of clothing to the survivors.
"'Look at this,' exclaimed
Loretta Rollock, 48 years old,
as she held up a green dress
and lingerie. 'I've never worn
such nice clothes. I feel like
when I was a kid and my mom
brought me something.' Then
she began to cry."

ii   In the Rubble

For some the hotel's collapse meant
life would have to be started
all over again.
Sixty-year-old Charles, on welfare
like so many of the others, who said,
'We are the rootless people,' and
'I have no home, no place that I can say I
really live in,' and,
'I had become used to it here,'
also said:
'I lost
all I ever had,
in the rubble.
I lost my clothes,
I lost the picture of my parents
and I lost my television.'

A Sound of Fear

There's a woman (you tell the gender by the noise of her heels)
lives in this 12-story building,
who won't use the elevator: hurries
down the emergency stairs from a floor higher than sixth
clop, clop, clop, every night
about the same time.
If I'm awake I hear her slowly
reascend
much later, pausing
to rest her legs
and breathe,
like someone climbing inside a monument
to see the view and say
I climbed it.
Every night.

Too Much to Hope

Twisted body and whitesocked
deformed legs (evidently
too hard to get stockings on).
And little, booted, braced, feet,
swinging along
beside the crutches and under
the huge winglike shoulders . . .

Always the tap and creak and
tap and creak of
crutch and brace,
in effort always, and whirr
of wings revving up and not
getting the human, female, botched body
off the ground.

The sound never
letting up, no hushed pinewoods walk,
no slipping unseen through lakes of shadow.
Has she
some blessed deafness given
along with starved bones?
                    It seems
too much to hope.

The Distance

While we lie in the road to block traffic from the air-force base,
over there the dead are strewn in the roads.

While we are carried to the bus and off to jail to be 'processed,'
over there the torn-off legs and arms of the living
hang in burnt trees and on broken walls.

While we wait and sing in ugly but not uninhabitable cells,
men and women contorted, blinded, in tiger cages, are
                                    biting their tongues
to stifle, for each other's sake, their cries of agony.
And those cruel cages are built in America.

While we refuse the standard prison liverwurst sandwiches,
knowing we'll get decent food in a matter of hours,
over there free fighters, young and old, guns never laid aside,
eat a few grains of rice and remember
Uncle Ho, and the long years he ate no better, and smile.

And while we fear
for the end of earth-life, even though we sing
and rejoice in each other's beauty and comradeship,

over there they mourn
the dead and mutilated each has seen.

16

They have seen and seen and heard and heard
all that we will ourselves with such effort to imagine,
to summon into the understanding . . .

And they too sing.
They too rejoice
in each other's beauty and comradeship:

they sing and fight. I see their spirits
visible, crowns of fire-thorn
flicker over their heads.

Our steps toward struggle
are like the first tottering of infant feet.
Could we,
          if life lasts
                    find in ourselves
that steady courage, win
such flame-crowns?

Weeping Woman

She is weeping for her lost right arm.
She cannot write the alphabet any more
on the kindergarten blackboard.

She is weeping for her lost right arm.
She cannot hold her baby and caress it at the same time
ever again.

She is weeping for her lost right arm.
The stump aches, and her side.

She is weeping for her lost right arm.
The left alone cannot use a rifle
to help shoot down the attacking plane.

In the wide skies over the Delta
her right hand that is not there
writes indelibly,
            'Cruel America,
when you mutilate our land and bodies,
it is your own soul you destroy,
not ours.'

The Pilots

Because they were prisoners,
because they were polite and friendly and lonesome and homesick,
because they said Yes, they knew
                        the names of the bombs they dropped
    but didn't say whether they understood what these bombs
                        are designed to do
                        to human flesh, and because
    I didn't ask them, being unable to decide
    whether to ask would serve
    any purpose other than cruelty, and
because since then I met Mrs. Brown, the mother of one of
                        their fellow prisoners,
and loved her, for she has the same lovingkindness in her
that I saw in Vietnamese women (and men too)
and because my hostility left the room and wasn't there
                        when I thought I needed it
while I was drinking tea with the POW's,

because of all these reasons I hope
they were truly as ignorant,
            as unawakened,
                        as they seemed,
I hope their chances in life up to this point
have been poor,
I hope they can truly be considered
victims of the middle America they come from,

18

their American Legionnaire fathers, their macho high schools,
their dull skimped Freshman English courses,

for if they did understand precisely
what they were doing, and did it anyway, and would do it again,

then I must learn to distrust
my own preference for trusting people,

then I must learn to question
my own preference for liking people,

then I must learn to keep
my hostility chained to me
so it won't leave me when I need it.

And if it is proved to me
that these men understood their acts,

how shall I ever again
be able to meet the eyes of Mrs. Brown?

A Place of Kindness

Somewhere there is a dull room
where someone slow is moving,
stumbling from door to chair

to sit there patiently
doing nothing but be,
enjoying the quiet and warmth,

pleased with the gradual
slope of day's light
into his corner. Dull

illiterate saint, never imagining
the atrocious skills his kin
devise and use,

who are avidly, viciously active,
refining quality, increasing quantity–
million by million–
of standardized Agony-Inflicters.

Somewhere there is a dull room
no phosphorescence of guile illumines.
No scintillations
of cruelty.

Imagination could put forth
gentle feelers there.
Somewhere there must be

such a room, and someone dumb
in it, unknown to cruelty,
unknowing.

May Our Right Hands Lose Their Cunning

Smart bombs replace
dumb bombs. 'Now we can aim
straight into someone's kitchen.'

Hard rice
sprays out of the cooking pot
straight into the delicate jelly of eyes.

Invisible pellets,
pointed blobs of mist,
     bite through smooth pale-brown skin
     into perfect bodies,

chewing them into bloody mincemeat.
This is smart.

There is
a dumb fellow, a mongoloid,
40 years old, who, being cherished,
learned recently to read and write,
and now has written a poem.
'Summer in the West when
everything is quiet
And clear, with everything
beautiful and green,
With wild flowers of all colors,
and a small water creek,
And a beautiful blue sky. And
the trees,' he wrote,
forming the letters carefully, his tongue
protruding, 'are very still.
And sometimes a small breeze.'

He has been cherished,
slowly learned
what many learn fast, and go on
to other knowledge. He
knows nothing of man's devices,
may die without discovering that
he's dumb, and they
are smart, the killers.

And the uncherished idiots,
tied in cots, smelling
of shit—
exquisite dumbness,
guaranteed not to know,
ever, how smart
a man can be,
homo faber of laser beams, of
quaintly-named, flesh-directed, utterly ingenious
mutilating spit-balls,

21

yes,
the smartest boys, obedient to all the rules, who never
aimed any flying objects across the classroom,
now are busy with finely calibrated equipment
fashioning spit-balls with needles in them,
that fly at the speed of light multiplied
around corners and into tunnels to arrive
directly at the dumb perfection of living targets,
icily into warm wholeness to fragment it.

We who
            know this
tremble
at our own comprehension.
Are we infected,
viciously, being smart enough
to write down these matters,
            scribes of the unspeakable?
We pray to retain
something round, blunt, soft, slow,
dull in us,
not to sharpen, not to be smart.

In Thai Binh (Peace) Province

for Muriel and Jane

I've used up all my film on bombed hospitals,
bombed village schools, the scattered
lemon-yellow cocoons at the bombed silk-factory,

and for the moment all my tears too
are used up, having seen today
yet another child with its feet blown off,
            a girl, this one, eleven years old,

patient and bewildered in her home, a fragile
small house of mud bricks among rice fields.

So I'll use my dry burning eyes
to photograph within me
dark sails of the river boats,
warm slant of afternoon light
apricot on the brown, swift, wide river,
village towers–church and pagoda–on the far shore,
and a boy and small bird both
perched, relaxed, on a quietly grazing
buffalo.   Peace within the
                    long war.

It is that life, unhurried, sure, persistent,
I must bring home when I try to bring
the war home.
                    Child, river, light.

Here the future, fabled bird
that has migrated away from America,
nests, and breeds, and sings,

common as any sparrow.

Fragrance of Life, Odor of Death

All the while among
the rubble even, and in
the hospitals, among the wounded,
                    not only beneath
                    lofty clouds

                              in temples
                    by the shores of lotus-dreaming
                    lakes

23

a fragrance:
flowers, incense, the earth-mist rising
of mild daybreak in the delta–good smell
of life.

It's in America
where no bombs ever
have screamed down smashing
the buildings, shredding the people's bodies,
tossing the fields of Kansas or Vermont or Maryland into
the air
to land wrong way up, a gash of earth-guts . . .
it's in America, everywhere, a faint seepage,
I smell death.

Hanoi-Boston-Maine, November 1972

A Poem at Christmas, 1972, during the Terror-Bombing of North Vietnam

Now I have lain awake imagining murder.
At first my pockets were loaded with rocks, with knives,
wherever I ran windows smashed, but I was swift
and unseen,
I was saving the knives until I reached
certain men . . .
Yes, Kissinger's smile faded,
he clutched his belly, he reeled . . .
But as the night
wore on, what I held
hidden–under a napkin perhaps,
I as a waitress at the inaugural dinner–
was a container of napalm:
and as I threw it in Nixon's face
and his crowd leapt back from the flames with crude
yells of horror,

and some came rushing to seize me:
          quick as thought I had ready
a round of those small bombs designed
to explode at the pressure of a small child's weight,
and these instantly
dealt with the feet of Nixon's friends and henchmen,
who fell in their own blood
while the foul smoke of his body-oils
blackened the hellish room . . .
It was of no interest
to imagine further. Instead,
the scene recommenced.
Each time around, fresh details,
variations of place and weapon.
All night imagining murder,
O, to kill
the killers!

It is
to this extremity

the infection of their evil

thrusts us . . .

Goodbye to Tolerance

Genial poets, pink-faced
earnest wits–
you have given the world
some choice morsels,
gobbets of language presented
as one presents T-bone steak
and Cherries Jubilee.
Goodbye, goodbye,
          I don't care

if I never taste your fine food again,
neutral fellows, seers of every side.
Tolerance, what crimes
are committed in your name.

And you, good women, bakers of nicest bread,
blood donors. Your crumbs
choke me, I would not want
a drop of your blood in me, it is pumped
by weak hearts, perfect pulses that never
falter: irresponsive
to nightmare reality.

It is my brothers, my sisters,
whose blood spurts out and stops
forever
because you choose to believe it is not your business.

Goodbye, goodbye,
your poems
shut their little mouths,
your loaves grow moldy,
a gulf has split
                    the ground between us,
and you won't wave, you're looking
another way.
We shan't meet again—
unless you leap it, leaving
behind you the cherished
worms of your dispassion,
your pallid ironies,
your jovial, murderous,
wry-humored balanced judgment,
leap over, un-
balanced? . . . then
how our fanatic tears
would flow and mingle
for joy . . .

January 1973

i

All the grievous wounds the murderers
crudely disguised as surgeons, inflict on the innocent–
gouging their flesh and the earth and rivers of their flesh–
are only debridements, light scrapings
of the layer just below the skin.

Breathing their own stale breath inside their masks,
fingers itching in bloody gloves,
they fail to touch the spirit-dragon
alive in the bone and marrow of their prey.

ii

From the Red River's many mouths
uprises
        a spirit-song.
Glittering drops that fall free from the nets
as fishermen take their catch
are the bright scales of the spirit-dragon.

iii

To live
beyond survival.
When a whole child
hurries to school with a legless child
on his back,
both of them flushed with pride,

the spirit-dragon
flies alongside them.

Hanoi, 1972–Temple, Maine, 1973

FIVE

Craving

Wring the swan's neck, seeking
a little language of drops of blood.

How can we speak of blood, the sky
is drenched with it.

A little language
of dew, then.

It dries.

A language
of leaves underfoot.
Leaves on the tree, trembling
in speech. Poplars
        tremble and speak
if you draw near them.

Dream Inscape

Mycelium, the delicate white threads
mushrooms weave in their chosen earth
(or manure or leafmold) to grow from

and milkweed silk orioles knit
into hammock nests their eggs
lilt in

and silver timbers
of old barns near salt water–

all of these
dreamed of, woven, knit, mitered
into a vision named 'A Visit Home'
(as if there were a home I had,
beyond the houses I live in, or those
I've lived in and hold
dimly in mind)
                    that waking
shook apart, out of
coherence, unwove, unraveled, took
beam by beam away, splintered.

The Way It Is

More real than ever, as I move
in the world, and never out of it,
Solitude.

Typewriter, telephone, ugly names
of things we use, I use. Among them, though,
float milkweed silks.

Like a mollusk's, my hermitage
is built of my own cells.
Burned faces, stretched horribly,

eyes and mouths forever open,
weight the papers down on my desk.
No day for years I have not thought of them.

And more true than ever the familiar image
placing love on a border
where, solitary, it paces, exchanging
across the line a deep attentive gaze
with another solitude pacing there.

Yet almost no day, too, with no
happiness, no
exaltation of larks uprising from the heart's
peat-bog darkness.

The Balance

At the door, some *never,* some *let it be,*
those pestering halftruths of impatience . . .

Yet the daily bread gets baked,
a rush of initiative takes the stairs
three at a time.
                            Crippled by their feet,
the swans waddle to water,
the first of them already
slowly and silently has ripped the silk of evening.

Cancion

When I am the sky
a glittering bird
slashes at me with the knives of song.

When I am the sea
fiery clouds plunge into my mirrors,
fracture my smooth breath with crimson sobbing.

When I am the earth
I feel my flesh of rock wearing down:
pebbles, grit, finest dust, nothing.

When I am a woman–O, when I am
a woman,
my wells of salt brim and brim,
poems force the lock of my throat.

SIX

The Woman

It is the one in homespun
you hunger for
when you are lonesome;

the one in crazy feathers
dragging opal chains in dust
wearies you

wearies herself perhaps
but has to drive on
clattering rattletrap into

fiery skies for trophies,
into the blue that is bluer
because of the lamps,

the silence keener because it is solitude
moving through multitude on the night streets.

But the one in homespun
whom you want is weary
too, wants to sit down

beside you neither silent
nor singing, in quietness. Alas,
they are not two but one,

pierce the flesh of one, the other
halfway across the world, will shriek,
her blood will run. Can you endure
life with two brides, bridegroom?

i

With dread she heard the letter
fall into the drop.

       Playing frisbee
         turns out to be a graceful merriment,
         almost like chasing butterflies.
Even she herself
could not have said for sure, as she played,
the letter was moving north already
to indict her history.

Decision, and fear, and then–
a picnic.
       'If I should come upon myself
suddenly,' she thinks, 'nothing would show I knew the
                    letter was crawling
grayly north to pronounce sentence,
to send a lifetime out into exile.'

       Magically the tangerine disc
         glides and curves and chooses
         to land in someone's outflung hand, sometimes
         even in unpracticed hers; gracious caprice.
Or circles back to fingers that sent it forth.
The game is a dance.
                Incandescent
the round charcoals, lambent
the white ash.
         Sun's fire
scatters between dark branches for those few
         passionate moments it takes each night to say
         farewell, and drop
                over the world's edge.
Laughter around the picnic table
lightly skims the ungathered dusk.

ii

Two letters passed each other, carried
north and south.
In the first was written: 'Our journey has come to a dead end,
we mustn't cower by that wall,
skin our fingers trying to scale it,
batter shoulder and head pushing against it,
perish there.
I have come to believe
it towers to the sky
and is thick through with layers of stone to the horizon.
We can only admit defeat,
and the road being closed to us by which we came—
closed like an ocean-furrow—
now we must each take one of the narrow paths,
left and right, parallel
to the wall at first,
then bearing away from it,
                              wider and wider apart
from it and from
each other.'
              In the second letter was written
'We must return
to sunrise and morning freshness, to seeing
one
another
anew.
        When I'm clear,
I see you, when I see you
I love you. How much life
we have lived together. Life begins
to wake new in me.'
The first letter is still
on its way, the second
has been received.
                    They are two songs
                    each in a different key,
                    two fables told

in different countries,
two pairs of eyes looking past each other
to different distances.

Summer 1972

Living for Two

Lily Bloom, what ominous fallen crowfeathers of shadow
the nightlight scattered around your outspread hair
on feverish cumulus of pillows–
demonic darkness, hair, feathers, jabs of greenish
sickroom light.
                    And your sallow face, long, lost, lonely,
O Lily Bloom, dying,
                    looked into mine those nights,
searching, equine, for life to be lived–
but not believing. Believing yourself fit for the knacker's yard . . .

What I told you–promised you–
though I meant it, didn't make sense:
Friendship, Life of Art, Love of Nature.
You had no correlatives, I had
no holiness.
You saved me the exact shame of not coming across. But Lily–
whom I remember not in my head (or barely once a year)
but in my nerves–what brimming measure of living
your death exacts from me! And when the fire of me smokes
or gasps as flames will do when a contending element
chokes their utterance, and they burn livid instead of red,

then I know I am cheating you. Living this half-life in my
                                        fiftieth year
cheats you. If I can't give you water, give myself
water, then I must give you, give myself, some icy spirits,
diamonds on the tongue,

                    to sear cracked lips and
                    quicken the heart: a ceremony
of living.
Love, lovers, husband, child, land and ocean, struggle and solitude:
you've had these, and more, but you need more.
                              We have other years
to go, Lily. I thirst too.
                    We're not free
of our covenant, Enemy, Burden, Friend.

Living Alone   **(I)**

In this silvery now of living alone,
doesn't it seem, I ponder,
anything can happen?
On the flat roof of a factory
at eye level from my window,
starling naiads dip in tremulous rainpools
where the sky floats, and is no smaller
than long ago.
Any strange staircase, as if I were twenty-one—
any hand drawing me up it,
could lead me to my life.
Some days.

And if I coast, down toward home, spring evenings, silently,
a kind of song rising in me to encompass
Davis Square and the all-night
cafeteria and the pool hall,
it is childhood's song, surely no note is changed,
sung in Valentines Park or on steep streets in the map of my mind
in the hush of suppertime, everyone gone indoors.
Solitude within multitude seduced me early.

Some days, though,
living alone,
there's only knowledge of silence,
clutter of bells cobwebbed
in crumbling belfry,
words jaggéd,
in midutterance broken.

Starlings, as before,
whistle wondering at themselves,
crescendo, diminuendo.
My heart pounds away,
confident as a clock.
Yet there is silence.

New leafed, the neighbor trees
round out. There's one,
near my window,
seems to have no buds, though.

Living Alone   (III)

I said, the summer garden I planted
bears only leaves–leaves in abundance–
but no flowers.
And then the flowers,
    many colors and forms,
    subtle, mysterious,
came forth.

I said, the tree has no buds.
And then the leaves,
    shyly, sparse, as if reluctant,

in less than two days appeared,
and the tree, now,
     is flying on green wings.

What magic denial
shall my life utter
to bring itself forth?

Cloud Poems

for Mitch

i.   **The Cloud**

We have entered sadness
as one enters a mountain cloud.

One stands in the midst of rain that is not raining.
Summits vanish, sheepdog's bark is dim.

Move and the cloud moves too,
and sighs with a million infinitesimal white breaths.

In single file, slowly,
clouds take to the sheep paths,

cloudy sadness, vague arms around us,
carries us like a bundle.

ii.   The Recollection

There was once a cloud–remember?
–with swift undulations drew away from our feet,
revealed that where we stood edged a precipice:

and deep below was a radiant valley,
rivers, fold and fields, gleaming villages.

iii.   The Cutting-beam

Imagine this blur of chill, white, gray, vague, sadness
burned off.

Imagine a landscape
of dry clear sunlight, precise shadows,
forms of pure color.

Imagine two neighboring hills, and
your house, my house, looking across, friendly:
imagine ourselves
meeting each other,
bringing gifts, bringing news.

Yes, we need the heat
of imagination's sun
to cut through our bonds of cloud.

And oh, can the great and golden light
warm our flesh that has grown so cold?

Don't You Hear That Whistle Blowin'. . .

The 4 a.m. freight comes pounding and shaking through
                                          the fall night
and I go to the Middle Door to watch,
                          through the plain glass that has
                                  stained glass around it,
pressing my forehead against the pane,

and Steve hurries along to look too–for he's out of Appalachia,
the lonesome romance of the rails West is in his bones;

and Richard comes close behind, gazing intently
                                          over my shoulder–
out of the Midwest and the rails West are in his blood,
and our friend Bo is at this very moment hopping freight in Oregon
                                          to pick pears;

and I seem to smell iron and rust, an animal smell,
                                          red and dusty,
even through the glass that's steaming up with our breaths.
So I start to open the door, to hear the last cars and the
                                          caboose louder
and the sound of going away, and to see the stars,

and I want you, Mitch, to step out with me into the dark garden,
for you're standing back of me too, taller than anyone;

but as the cold air comes in I turn toward you and you're
                                          not there.
Then I realize I'm waking up: the train really is going by
but the Middle Door's back in my childhood, not in America,

and there's no one in the house but you and me,
you asleep beside me in bed, and soon you'll have left
and this moment of dark boxcars just visible
under the paling stars, a train of looming forms from
                                                    faraway states
lurching through the edge of Boston,

is just the beginning of a long train of times I'll turn
to share a vision with you and find I'm dreaming.

September 6–7, 1974

Divorcing

One garland
of flowers, leaves, thorns
was twined round our two necks.
Drawn tight, it could choke us,
yet we loved its scratchy grace,
our fragrant yoke.

We were Siamese twins.
Our blood's not sure
if it can circulate,
now we are cut apart.
Something in each of us is waiting
to see if we can survive,
severed.

Strange Song

A virtuoso dog at midnight–high wavering howl
resolved in three staccato low barks.
Three times the same utterance
repeated, insisted on.
It makes sure, like a bird practicing,
                    through the day,
                        its phrase.
I listen half asleep, aware
of pleasure in listening,
not afraid of my solitude.
Yet the fear nags me: is the wound
my life has suffered
                        healing too fast,
shutting in bad blood?
Will the scar
pucker the skin of my soul?
'Shut up,' someone shouts at the dog
who again lifts his complaint
into the fall night in strange song.

Grief

When your voice breaks
I'm impaled on the jaggéd
edges of its fracture.

It is visible
to mind's eye, bone or grained
splintering wood.

Bone-voice, O wooden
sobbing. The flesh of my spirit
is sore. I'm powerless

to mend you. Marrow,
or sap rising in the fibers
that hold, must do it.

I suffer
less your pain than my
helplessness,

hoisted off the
earth of my energies like
a bug overturned,

feet waving
wild and feeble.

Libation

Raising our glasses, smilingly
we wish one another not luck
but happiness. After half a lifetime
with and without luck,
we know we need more than luck.
It makes no difference that we're drinking
tomato juice, not wine or whiskey–
we know what we mean,
and the red juice of those virtuous
vegetable-fruits is something we both enjoy.
I remember your wonder, as at a miracle,
finding them growing on sturdy vines
in my old aunt and uncle's sun-room
ripe to pluck at the breakfast table!
We were twenty-three, and unappeasably hungry . . .

We agree on tomatoes, then–and happiness?
yes, that too: we mean growth, branching,
leafing, yielding blossoms and fruit and the sharp odor

                                        of dreams.
We mean knowing someone as deeply,
no, deeper, than we've known each other,
we mean being known. We are wishing each other
the luck not to need luck. I mill
some pepper into my juice, though,
and salt in the ancient gesture; and what would be wrong
with tipping out half a glass
for the gods?
                        We smile.
After these months of pain we begin
to admit our new lives have begun.

February 1975

SEVEN

Seth Thomas: A Love Poem

for Fran and Tom

Rejoining Time after fifty years,
not slow, not fast.
Pendulum beaming gold in miniature cupboard.
Confident lame tock *tock*.
Melodious chime of three at one a.m.,
midnight at seven.

The Quality of Genius

i

Trees that lift themselves like clouds
above the woods,

crest of the woods and then
more, a breath

in winter air, a web
of fiber, from afar

so tenuous, near
a stiff hard complication

of live sticks.

ii

Eve's lavender
from a garden gone
        seven years now
under concrete–

fragrant.
        (The church wanted
        money: but Eve,
    moneyless, with a poet's
    humor, or lack of it,

    did not waste the pink
    Thank Offering envelope,
    'To Be Used Any Time God Has Blessed You,'

    ideal for mailing lavender,
    mint leaves, or winged seeds

    when the spirit
        moved her.)

iii

Encircling gold faded
to gray, stalks
tough still but leaves
frost bitten,

what large brown faces
–smiling,
seedy–
the sunflowers have.

iv

Which of them has it
it's too soon to tell–

David, John,
    Naomi, Carlene . . .

Confusion, growth, the analogies
perceived.   Seed of words
that didn't come up three
or five or seven
years back putting out
green shoots now, small
sturdy shrubs, vine tangles not resembling
remembered cotyledons.
                          Paul, Andrea, Aaron . . .
Letters
come in from
              far away
as if in bottles.
            (What was
the ancient children's game,
some token
concealed and passed
from hand to hand? Pincushion, button, ring–
some common
talisman . . .)

Flames upspring
feline
      to illumine
one face or another, moments
of profound chiaroscuro,
definition of feature–

but not yet
from inside out through their skulls
or through one skull
persistently

the fiery moonlight,
     the tattered rage
     of the sun . . .

Growth of a Poet

i

He picks up crystal buttons from the ocean floor.
Gills of the mind pulse in unfathomed water.

In the infinite dictionary he discovers
gold grains of sand. Each has its twin
on some shore the other side of the world.

Blind to what he does not yet need,
he feels his way over broken glass
to the one stone that fits his palm.

When he opens his eyes he gives to what he gazes at
the recognition no look ever before granted it.
It becomes a word. Shuddering, it takes wing.

ii

> 'What is to give light must endure burning.'
> Viktor Frankl, *The Doctor and the Soul*

Blind until dreaming gray
sparks green, his eyes
set fire to an ashen street,
a dancer's
bitter flesh in daybreak,
the moon's

last noontime look
over its shoulder.
They fade; the flames
go on burning,
enduring.

iii

Deaf till he hears
what answers:
                    Grandfatherly
bell, tolling
and telling
of faithful Time, that flood
(ever-rolling), of faithful blood.
The answers pushing
boundaries over,
(those proud embankments),
the asking revealed.

The asking, stones
bared of earth,
hammers at the door, a pulse
in the temple:
the insistent dance
of Who and How and Where,
the arms-akimbo of When.

iv

One at a time
books, when their hour is come
step out of the shelves.
Heavily step (once more, dusty, fingermarked,
                    but pristine!)
to give birth:

each poem's passion
ends in an Easter,
a new life.

        The books of the dead
shake their leaves,
word-seeds fly and
lodge in the black earth.

v

Coffee cups fall out of his hands,
doorknobs slip his grasp and
doors slam,
antique writing desks break under his
leaning elbows–Taurus
is bucking and thudding, head down across
the cramped field.
                But scraps of wood
found on the street, one night when winds were
scraping the thick dark to a steely shine,
              become in the poet's hands
a table,
      round and
set firm on its one leg.

vi

To make poems is to find
an old chair in the gutter
and bring it home
into the upstairs cave;
a stray horse from the pound,
a stray boat on the weedy shore,
phosphorescent.

Then in the broken rocking chair
take off—to reality!
Realm of ambrosia and hard crusts
earnest trudging doesn't lead to.

Only when feet begin
to dance, when the chair
creaks and gallops,
do the gates open
and we
          discover ourselves
inside
the kingless kingdom.

vii

The wild moonbull
                    who is the poet
grazes alone
a field of infinite, dewdrenched,
drops of red clover,
sharp spears of grass
                    which are words

Over the barbed fence a troop
of boys and young men
                    who are the poet
throng,
          breathless, silent,
to the encounter.

They desire
to practice the dance.
Secretly to prepare.
He breathes
his green, fresh, breath at them,
still distant,
gazing innocent

through full-moon silver
toward them
and viciously
rushes them, they step
each aside,
old coats for capes,
they taunt him,
he tosses
his deadly flourish of horns,
they love him, they imagine
the hot sunlight of the sacred kill.

Implacable silver
fades. By moonset

they vanish, he hears
the wire fence
twang where they climbed it.

viii

Shadowdog
blocking the threshold.
Only a shadow. But
bites!
      Try
to get out, try
to get in:
         the obstacle
sinks its
teeth in
flesh, and

blood flows,
they are not
shadowteeth,
are sharp, and
dirty.

The venom rises
from torn foot to
heart. Makes
a knot in the heart.

A screeching:
of brakes on the street,
of an unsuspected
voice outcrying
through the poet's
lips, denying
poetry,
          violent
palpitating beat of
the mind's wings caged.

Dust on the tongue.

Storm
of torn feathers.

Falling.
          Falling–

ix

Hassidic rocking
is always back and forth,
          back and forth,
in perfect measure with the words,
over and over,
every day of the year–

except one:

on the day the Temple is destroyed
        which is also
the day the Messiah is born,
on that day alone, the rocking
moves from side to side,
                side to side,
a swaying,
as trees sway in the wind.

x

On his one leg that aches
the poet
learns to stand firm
upholding
the round table of his
blank page.
When the wind blows
his wood
shall be tree again.
Shall stir,
shall sigh and sing.

xi

> 'Whatever has black sounds, has *duende.*'
> *Manuel Torres, quoted by Federico García Lorca*

And now the sounds
are green, a snowdrop's quiet
defiant insignia:

and now the sounds
crackle with mica glitterings,
rasp with cinder,
call with the oboe calm of rose quartz:

and now the sounds
are bone flutes, echo
from deepest canyon, sounds
only the earliest, palest stars may hear:

and now the sounds
are black. Are black sounds.
Black. The deep song
delves.

Conversation in Moscow

Red wine
        from the
                Black Sea.
                        Glasses
filled and refilled,
Georgian shishkebab has been eaten,
                        plates pushed back, voices
of other diners surround us–

Sometimes the five of us speak at once, so much is lost,
                                        we are all
in our forties, it is perhaps ten at night–

the woman who is
                our interpreter
                knows, she knows
poignantly: now is the night she must speak for us–

People look round to see who's come in, all
members of the tribe of the word. Chairs are pushed back,
                                        swing door
lets out moments of kitchen clatter–
                        She knows she must *be*

each of us turn by turn and
each at once.

I see their eyes:

The fat poet I barely know, but surely
love,
who pours the wine
quietly, his eyes
kind, small, and sorrowful.
Blue, blue eyes in a tanned face, the veriest *azure* eyes
I've looked to ever: the poet's trusted friend; historian,
fresh from the re-examined lives of the Nihilists.

(Will you have ice cream?–the waiters
returning and leaving again)–

                        Pale eyes of the biologist, pale face,
white beard,
though not old. He's O.K.,
a good guy–
but the others
know things he doesn't know.
He has
an aura of limits . . .

And I, I'm looking
from one to the other, trying to read
language in gesture, grasping
what Russian words I know, turning
to her who so often
looks either acutely anxious or deeply amused–
my sister the medium-interpretress! Oracle!–to give me
what these brothers are saying (for there's a spirit
has touched us, pulled us
suddenly close).

                  Frown-lines and laugh-lines leave her face,
she is looking

56

                    upward through smoke to the high ceiling,
                            and through it
                              searching–

'Each cell,' the biologist says, 'has in it
the whole body's potential.'
                        (And I think of the module, of detail
                            giving to inscape its signature, the great
                                web of analogy)–
but it seems he implies
some kind of determinism (I've been saying
I don't see *enough* communism here, no struggling toward
a classless society). Communism to him
is only the best we can do
with the historic, the social, shell, in which
the creature lives
                    unregenerate.
                            The historian faults him,
but I lose that, people come by, greetings exchanged–

Red wine from the black sea.
She searches
and finds the eloquent, accurate words of translation:
                                    the poet now
out of his stillness is talking: 'Poems,' he says,
'poems are of two kinds: those with mystery,
                            those without mystery.'
'And are poems without mystery poems at all?' 'Well . . . yes;
one cannot say
a poem wellmade, effective, but unmysterious,
has no value. But for myself–
I prefer the mysterious . . .'
                            'And Dostoyevsky–
why is it he, who's so often
clearly reactionary, pessimistic, all for
personal redemption and against
common action–antirevolutionary!–why is it he's
the 19th-century writer I see is most read, most loved,
in the Soviet Union?–Whereas Turgeniev, for instance,

whose work surely–(I think of the *Sportsman's Sketches*
                                        especially)–'
'*Ah!* But Dostoyevsky!' (Historian and poet, both are speaking)
'Who reached as he did into the hot and strange–'
                                'the cold and shadowy–'
'the intricate depths of life? We read him–'
                                        'We read him because:
in him–'
        '–in him we know
our own darknesses and illuminations,
tortures and ecstasies: our human reality.'

Tea in glasses. Thick black coffee. Vodka? Vodka.
'To *Serve the People,*' I venture, 'is often thought of
–wrongly, narrowly–merely as mutual encouragement.
But to serve the people in truth one must do, I think,
what Pasternak said one must do: *excel oneself
in order to be oneself.*'
                        'To serve the people,' (the poet again
holds us in his hands, we are listening shells to whom
a heartbeat speaks),
                        'to serve the people
one must write for the ideal reader. Only for the ideal reader.
And who or what is that ideal reader? God. One must imagine,
one must deeply *imagine*
                        that great Attention.
Only so,
in lonely dialogue, can one reach–
the people.'

After our musing silences
have traveled away, each on its own road,
and returned again to this night, this place
of meeting–island of our eternity in the bustle and clatter
of passing time–now the biologist
(pale, skeptical, yet a friend: I see he's at bottom innocent
as only the trained skeptic can be,
whose imagination
is weak as fine hair) is telling,

when I've asked if anyone reads Kropotkin, that,
'Lenin said, after he'd talked for hours with Kropotkin,
What a charming old man! and shook his head, and added,
But he understands nothing. Nothing. But later Lenin sent
a train, a special train back and forth to the place where he,
the old man, lay dying, only to ask each day after him . . .'

He smiles, he is pale and gentle.
                              'To me it seems,'
I say, going slowly, waiting for her: she's ready:
'To me it seems perhaps
Kropotkin understood half
                              of what we need to know,
and Lenin perhaps
knew half, and true revolution . . . true revolution
must put these two halves together?'

                    A flash
                    of sapphire!
          I hear
          the historian's words, and understand them,
          and wonder:
my woman friend
repeats in English, 'How young! How pure!'

I'm abashed, though he is speaking
without mockery, almost tenderly.
                              'I young, pure? Why, I'm two years older
than our friend here, the poet . . . And what have I spoken of
but doubts, of perplexity?'
'Human doubts, human longing,' he utters the words
solemnly,–'human longing
                              for ineffable justice and mercy:
in these lies purity
and the worth of men's lives–
new as a birch bud in spring.'

          His mind has touched, moved into and out of,
              as if into seacarved hollows bristling with hidden spines,

59

                              venomous tentacles,
                    the life of Nechaev,
                    killer, shaman. He has known
                    the sacrament of the absolute.

          And then he says,
                              'In the end
we must follow Christ.' 'Is he joking?'–
                              I turn to my woman friend again, confused.
'No. No,' the historian says, understanding my question,
'I am not joking. I'm speaking
of spirit. Not dogma but spirit. The Way.'

                              (Not the corrupt Church–
                    bejeweled priests with dirty beards
                    prostrating themselves before the atrocious Czars–
its indispensable beggars encrusting the entrances
of every shrine, kissing with pus
the infinite insensibility of relics.

                    Not this but
                    the frail trust we have
                    when our hearts flutter, and we look
                    each to each,
                    and our eyes hold.
                              The Way.)
And the poet–it's midnight, the room is half empty, soon
                              we must part–
the poet, his presence
ursine and kind, shifting his weight in a chair too small
                              for him,
quietly says, and shyly: 'The Poet
                    never must lose despair.'
Then our eyes indeed
meet and hold.
          All of us know, smiling
in common knowledge–
even the palest spirit among us, burdened
as he is with weight of abstractions–

all of us know he means
we mustn't, any of us, lose touch with the source,
pretend it's not there, cover over
the mineshaft of passion
                    despair somberly tolls its bell
                              from the depths of,

and wildest joy
sings out of too,
                flashing
                      the scales of its laughing, improbable
                                            music,

grief and delight entwined in the dark down there.

'The Poem Rising By Its Own Weight'

> The poet is at the disposal of his own night.
> *Jean Cocteau*

The singing robes fly onto your body and cling there silkily,
you step out on the rope and move unfalteringly across it,

and seize the fiery knives unscathed and
keep them spinning above you, a fountain
of rhythmic rising, falling, rising
flames,

and proudly let the chains
be wound about you, ready
to shed them, link by steel link,
padlock by padlock–

                but when your graceful
confident shrug and twist drives the metal
into your flesh and the python grip of it tightens

and you see rust on the chains and blood in your pores
and you roll
over and down a steepness into a dark hole
and there is not even the sound of mockery in the distant air
somewhere above you where the sky was,
no sound but your own breath panting:
then it is that the miracle
walks in, on his swift feet,
down the precipice straight into the cave,
opens the locks,
knots of chain fall open,
twists of chain unwind themselves,
links fall asunder,
in seconds there is a heap of scrap-
metal at your ankles, you step free and at once
he turns to go—

but as you catch at him with a cry,
clasping his knees, sobbing your gratitude,
with what radiant joy he turns to you,
and raises you to your feet,
and strokes your disheveled hair,
and holds you,
                    holds you,
                                holds you
close and tenderly before he vanishes.

EIGHT

Prayer for Revolutionary Love

That a woman not ask a man to leave meaningful work to
follow her.
That a man not ask a woman to leave meaningful work to
follow him.

That no one try to put Eros in bondage.
But that no one put a cudgel in the hands of Eros.

That our loyalty to one another and our loyalty to our work
not be set in false conflict.

That our love for each other give us love for each other's work.
That our love for each other's work give us love for one another.

That our love for each other's work give us love for one another.
That our love for each other give us love for each other's work.

That our love for each other, if need be,
give way to absence. And the unknown.

That we endure absence, if need be,
without losing our love for each other.
Without closing our doors to the unknown.

Modes of Being

for Nguyen Cong Hoan

January's fist
unclenches.
　　　Walls of brick
are bastions of coral, welltempered, basking,
and shadows yawn and
stretch to the east.
　　　Watching the afternoon,
from the window watching it slowly brim
and not spill, not yet, into evening,
soothes and gives pleasure.

> *Near Saigon,*
> *in a tiger-cage, a man*
> *tries to stretch out his hand*
> *and cannot.*

Indoors, reading, talking,
we reach and enter
　　　a new landscape of knowledge,
as if coming through a high mountain pass together,
that wonder of other flora, different
ways of constructing rooves and
terracing fields, the haymakers
dressed differently.
　　　What more
can love be than epiphany!

> *Near Saigon,*
> *in a tiger-cage, a woman*
> *tries to straighten her*
> 　　　*cramped spine*
> *and cannot.*

64

Unclenched fist,
cinnamon warmth of winter light,
revelation, communion . . .
Unable
          to know for long
what we know; neither intense love
nor intense pain. Nature itself
allows the delight of sparrows
ruffling an inchdeep lake of rain
in the jailhouse yard.
                              Joy
is real, torture
is real, we strain to hold
a bridge between them open,
and fail,
or all but fail.

          *Near Saigon, in cages
          made in America, jailers
          force fluid down the prisoners' throats,
          stomp on their swollen bellies.
          This has been happening
          for a long time.
          This is happening
          now, while I write, January
          nineteen seventy-four.*

What wings, what mighty arch
of feathered hollow bones, beyond
span of albatross or eagle,
mind and heart must grow
                              to touch, trembling,
with outermost pinion tips,
not in alternation but both at once,
in one
violent eternal instant
that which is and
that which is . . .

A Letter to Marek about a Photograph

for Mark Pawlak

This carpentered, unpainted, aging house,
one of many alike in some white ghetto,
is filled to the uninsulated seams with a face:
the brooding face of anxiety.   –Or the house
(one cannot say which is
superimposed on the other) is so montaged,
waking and sleeping, into that mind, it is
the house fills the outgazing head,
extends its boundaries with wooden angles.
                              And the face
is the face of your father, Marek,
a Polish workman, or of his brother, or–
for, beardless and hair dragged back,
it could be the face of a woman–your mother,
your grandmother in the 1930's,
just staying off the breadline . . .
any young woman quickly grown old, forehead
deeply wrinkled, eyes unable to laugh. Whatever else
–store-boughten furnishings, tawdry treasures, stories–
is inside the house, at the door
that *look* looks out,
worry without hope.
                              But the house itself
though cheaply built, has its share of ornaments turned on the lathe
of humor and trust, a human, unique
identity fronting the weather. In houses like these
your family of millions, Polacks, Wops,
Scotch-Irish, people shut now into 'projects,'
used to live. You would have known its
familiar mystery, its faint, sour charm,
even by dark, even before you had seen
its fretted gable, Marek:
your in-feeling comprehension
would touch with probing finger
the concealed wounds of those who built,

those who dwelt, those who moved on
or died here. Your gift is to reveal
poetry in the cries caught in nameless throats,
in eyes gazing into the street of trouble,
and foolish tender joys suspended
in half-light of memory; to lift
griefs out of the blind pit of unknowing,
placing glass and mercury under the tongue of dreams–
magical quick–
silver that measures
the fever it is to be human.

Room

for D. Mitchell and D. Hass

Shelf of worn, chipped, exquisite china oddments,
for daily use.
Baskets, for fruit, potatoes, shopping.
Stove with grill where David
makes such good brown toast.
Left of the sink, above the counter,
Mary Wollstonecraft, fair face, dark shadows, energy.
Slightly unsteady, the small table. Notes to each other,
and soon, when David and David come home,
strong cups of tea.
It's the kitchen, its window viewless,
and not the handsome calm of the living room,
I find myself in, at peace,
though the presence across the hall of
that room too is part of being here:
the threadbare gracious carpet,
surreal romances of the Victorian *découpage* screen,
poplars and oaks and sunsets the large windows look to.
Afternoon, an ample easy quiet.
                                But it breaks
sharply: the Davids

have moved, all the objects
stand at new angles, a kitchen I've never seen,
light from another compass point.
This room, my refuge, is nowhere but in my mind,
more blurred for them than for me, their memories
too many to sift and focus. 'Bees of the invisible,'
take this nectar, transform it, internalize it! If I lose
the knowledge of this place,
my soul shall be diminished. There is a song in all
humankind, that rooms, houses, parks, streets, fields
and particular corners of fields, rivers and certain
eye-span reaches of rivers, are notes in, as people are.
Give me the power
to sound this note, the disappeared-
as-if-torn-down, but clear, cool, tranquil kitchen
on Downside Crescent present in me,
a place to *be* in, not pretending
no tears were shed in it, no hard words ever shouted,
no gray mornings caught in the small mirror over the sink—
but seeing despite that, precisely because of that,
(grief not being turned away, a place
made for grief to be) one could
be there, and breathe easy, uncrowded.
A note or chord of notes
sustained, hushing, recurrent
in the stream of song.

Voyage

for Barbara Fussiner and Richard Edelman

Fluttering strips of paper strung on cord
tied to the ship's rail.
Each inscribed.
Read them:

'How deep the waves' blue!'

'How bright the foam!'

'Wind and light
sparkle together!'

'How the sea's plumage
preens itself!'

These are prayers.
To celebrate,
not to beseech.
Among them, leaning
toward the water, we voyage,
are voyaged, seeing.
We share among us
the depth of day, are borne
through it
swiftly as arcs of spray.

Salt glitters
on our lips,
on ruffled paper. Soon
the words will fly on their torn strips
beyond vision.

        Silent, smiling, receiving
joyfully what we are given,
we utter
each to each
our absolute presence.

NINE

Waving to the Devil

Tasted (and spat out)
Satan's Boletus.
Delicious!

Consulting the Oracle

I asked a blind man the way east,
because I'd not seen him,
not looked before asking.
He smiled, and walked on,
sure of his felt way,
silent.

The Life of Others

Their high pitched baying
as if in prayer's unison

remote, undistracted, given over
utterly to belief,

the skein of geese
voyages south,
            hierarchic arrow of its convergence toward
            the point of grace
swinging and rippling, ribbon tail
of a kite, loftily

over lakes where they have not
elected to rest,

over men who suppose
earth is man's, over golden earth

preparing itself
for night and winter.
                        We humans
are smaller than they, and crawl
unnoticed,

about and about the smoky map.

Freedom

Perhaps we humans
have wanted God most as witness
to acts of choice
made in solitude. Acts of mercy,
of sacrifice. Wanted
that great single eye to see us,
steadfast as we flowed by.
Yet there are other acts
not even vanity,
or anxious hope to please, knows of—
bone doings, leaps of nerve, heart—
cries of communion: if there is bliss,
it has
been already
and will be; out-
reaching, utterly.
Blind
to itself, flooded
with otherness.

Unwrap the dust from its mummycloths.
Let Ariel learn
a blessing for Caliban
and Caliban drink dew from the lotus
open upon the waters.
Bitter the slow
river water: dew
shall wet his lips with light.
Let the dust
float, the wrappings too
are dust.
          Drift upon the stir
of air, of dark
river: ashes of what had lived,
                    or seeds
          of ancient sesame,
                    or namelessly
pure dust that is all
in all.   Bless,
weightless Spirit. Drink,
Caliban, push your tongue
heavy into the calyx.

The Wealth of the Destitute

How gray and hard the brown feet of *the wretched of the earth.*
How confidently the crippled from birth
push themselves through the streets, deep in their lives.
How seamed with lines of fate the hands
of women who sit at streetcorners
offering seeds and flowers.
How lively their conversation together.
How much of death they know.
I am tired of 'the fine art of unhappiness.'

LIFE IN THE FOREST (1978)

'We work in the dark. We do what we can. We give what we have. Our doubt is our passion. Our passion is our task. The rest is the madness of art.'

Henry James

In 1975 or '6 I found in Cesare Pavese's poems of the 1930's, *Lavorare Stanca,* read in the Penguin edition translated by Margaret Crosland, a kind of ratification for a direction I was already obscurely taking in my own work. Pavese's beautiful poems are about various persons other than himself; though he is a presence in them also, their focus is definitely not autobiographical and egocentric, and in his accompanying essays he speaks of his concept of suggesting a narrative through the depiction of a scene, a landscape, rather than through direct recounting of events as such. The poems I had been moving towards were impelled by two forces: first, a recurring need–dealt with earlier by resort to a diarylike form, a poem long enough to include prose passages and discrete lyrics–to vary a habitual lyric mode; not to abandon it, by any means, but from time to time to explore more expansive means; and second, the decision to try to avoid overuse of the autobiographical, the dominant first-person singular of so much of the American poetry–good and bad–of recent years.

Those poems of my own which have, I feel, some humble affinity–however oblique–with what Pavese achieved in *Lavorare Stanca,* tend to rather long lines and a discursive structure. The content of the last five of them is, however, shared by certain other poems–the first three of *Continuum*–that do not belong, in tone and structure, to the *Homage to Pavese* section of this book. This is not wholly true of 'A Soul-Cake': formally it could belong with the *Homage to Pavese* poems; but its more emphatic use of the first person unfits it for that group. By placing it, together with 'A Visit' and 'Death Psalm,' at the beginning of *Continuum,* I hope to suggest to the reader alternative ways of reading all eight poems–i.e., they can be considered as belonging to their respective sections, or they can be read as an internal grouping that spans the two sections.

The poem in *Homage to Pavese* called 'Chekhov on the West Heath' grew out of being asked to contribute something to the Chekhov Festival organized by James McConkey at Cornell University early in 1977. Though originally I had considered presenting a prose piece I found myself stimulated into a poem. In this instance I felt that, despite the frankly autobiographical standpoint taken, the poem belonged in the 'Pavese' section by virtue of its focus on other persons and on place.

The group called *Modulations for Solo Voice* appeared in a limited edition published by Five Trees Press in San Francisco as a benefit to provide funds for publication of a young, unknown, woman poet. These poems are definitely a sequence, and make the most sense read in the order in which they are arranged–which, however, differs from that of their original printing in one particular: the last two poems are reversed, what was originally called 'Litany' now becoming the coda or 'Epilogue.'

Throughout the rest of the book the arrangement is less chronological than by kind and, within such kinship groups, by internal association from poem to poem.

Human Being

Human being–walking
in doubt from childhood on: walking

a ledge of slippery stone in the world's woods
deep-layered with wet leaves–rich or sad: on one
side of the path, ecstasy, on the other
dull grief.   Walking

the mind's imperial cities, roofed-over alleys,
                        thoroughfares, wide boulevards
that hold evening primrose of sky in steady calipers.

Always the mind
walking, working, stopping sometimes to kneel
in awe of beauty, sometimes leaping, filled with the energy
of delight, but never able to pass
the wall, the wall
of brick that crumbles and is replaced,
of twisted iron,
of rock,
the wall that speaks, saying monotonously:

        Children and animals
                        who cannot learn
        anything from suffering,
        suffer, are tortured, die
        in incomprehension.

This human being, each night nevertheless
summoning–with a breath blown at a flame,
                        or hand's touch
on the lamp-switch–darkness,
                silently utters,

79

impelled as if by a need to cup the palms
and drink from a river,
                              the words, 'Thanks.
Thanks for this day, a day of my life.'
                                        And wonders.
Pulls up the blankets, looking
into nowhere, always in doubt.
And takes strange pleasure
in having repeated once more the childish formula,
a pleasure in what is seemly.
And drifts to sleep, downstream
on murmuring currents of doubt and praise,
the wall shadowy, that tomorrow
will cast its own familiar, chill, clear-cut shadow
into the day's brilliance.

Writing to Aaron

. . . after three years–a 3-decker novel
in fifteen pages? Which beginning
to begin with? 'Since I saw you last,
the doctor has prescribed me artificial tears,
a renewable order . . .' But that leaves out
the real ones. Shall I write about them?
What about comedy, laughter, good news?
'I live in a different house now,
but can give you news
of most of the same people . . .' That ignores
the significance of the house, its tone of voice,
and the sentence by sentence
unfolding of lives into chapters.
'Your last letter told about sand-dunes in winter,
and having the sea to yourself.
Beautiful; I read it to the strangers
in whose midst I was at the time.
And that's the way we lost touch for so long,

my response was the reading aloud
instead of a letter,
and we both moved house–
a shifting of sand underfoot . . .'

Well, I could echo
the sound of facts, their weather–
thunderclaps, rain hitting stone, rattle of windows.
And spaces would represent sunlight,
when the wind gave over and everyone rested
between the storms.
Or chronological narrative? 'In the spring
of '73,' . . . 'That summer,'
'By then it was fall . . .'
                 All or nothing–
and that would be nothing,
dust, parchment dried up, invisible ink.
Maybe I'll leave the whole story
for you to imagine,
telling you only, 'A year ago,
I said farewell to that poplar you will remember,
that gave us its open secret,
pressed on us all we could grasp, and more,
of vibrating, silvergreen being,
a tree tripping over its phrases in haste,
eloquent aspen.'

I know you know
it took my farewell for granted:
what it had given, it would never take back.
I know you know
about partings, tears, eyedrops, revisions, dwellings,
                               discoveries,
mine or yours; those are the glosses,
Talmudic tractates, a lifetime's study. The Word itself
is what we heard, and shall always hear, each leaf
imprinted, syllables in our lives.

Tough guy. Star of David
and something in Hebrew—a motto—
hang where Catholics used to dangle
St. Christopher (now discredited).
No smile. White hair. American-born,
I'd say, maybe the Bronx.
When another cab pulls alongside
at a light near the Midtown Tunnel, and its driver
rolls down his window and greets this guy
with a big happy face and a first-name greeting,
he bows like a king, a formal acknowledgement,
and to me remarks,
                deadpan,
            'Seems to think he knows me.'

'You mean you don't know him?'—I lean forward laughing,
close to the money-window.
                    'Never seen him before in my life.'
Something like spun steel floats invisible, until
                      questions strike it,
all round him, the way light gleams webs among
                        grass in fall.
And on we skim
in silence past the cemeteries, into
the airport, ahead of time. He's beat
the afternoon traffic. I tip him well.
A cool acceptance. Cool? It's
cold as ice.

        Yet I've seen,
squinting to read his license,
how he smiled—timidly?—anyway,
smiled, as if hoping to please,
at the camera. My heart

stabs me. Somewhere this elderly
close-mouthed skeptic hides
longing and hope. Wanted
–immortalized for the cops, for his fares, for the world–
to be looking his best.

Nightingale Road

How gold their hair was,
and how their harps
and sweet voices called out into the valley
summer nights!

The boys black-haired,
coming home black with coal dust, same as us all,
but milk-skinned when they'd had their wash.
One of the boys, Arthur,
went down the pit the first time
same day as me.

And the girls–that gold hair
twining like pea-vine tendrils,
and even the youngest could play her harp.

Up on the mountain their house was,
up Nightingale Street, and then as you leave the village
it's Nightingale Road.
Mother and father, the three boys
and the six girls; all of them singing,
you'd think the gates of Heaven were open.

And funny thing–
the T.B. didn't stop them
each one, till a few weeks only
before it took them.
One by one
the whole family went, though.

Oh, but the sound was fine!
I'd be a young boy, lying awake,
and I'd smell my Mam's
honeysuckle she'd got growing
up the house wall, and I'd hear them singing,
a regular choir they were,
and the harps rippling out

and somehow as I'd be falling asleep
I couldn't tell which was the music
and which was that golden hair they had,
and all with that milky skin. The voices
sweet and gold and shrill and the harps
flowing like milk.

S. Wales, circa *1890*

Chekhov on the West Heath*

for Jim McConkey
who spurred me into writing it
and for Rebecca Garnett
who was and is 'Bet'

A young girl in a wheelchair,
another girl pushing the chair.
Up from Heath Mansions they go,
past the long brick wall of the Fenton House garden.
The invalid girl's hands move as she speaks, delicately,
describing the curve of a cloud.
The other, younger one comes into focus;
how could I know so well
the back of my own head? I could touch the hair
of the long plait . . . Ah,
that's it: the young girl painting
in Corot's *L'Atelier,* upright, absorbed,
whose face we don't see. *There I am,*
I thought, the first time I saw it,
startled.
Up through small streets they go,
the crest of the hill, a stonesthrow of unpaved lane,
and out to the terrace: a few
lopsided benches, tussocky grass,
and the great billowing prospect north.
This is Hampstead. This
is Judge's Walk. It is nineteen hundred
and forty-one.
The war? They take it for granted;
it was predicted while they were children,
and has come to pass. It means
no more ballet school, Betty is ill,
I am beginning to paint in oils.
The war is simply

* See notes on page 275.

how the world is, to which they were born.
They share
  the epiphanies of their solitudes,
hardly knowing or speaking to anyone else
their own age. They have not discovered men
or sex at all. But daily
they live! Live
intensely. Mysterious fragrance
gentles the air
under the black poplars.
And Bet, looking off towards hawthorn and willow,
middle-distance of valley and steep small hills,
says she would like to bounce
from one round-topped tree to another,
in the spring haze.

Often and often, as they talk and gaze,
that year and the next,
                    Chekhov is with them.
With us.
      The small, dark-green volumes.
      The awkward, heroic versions.
We're not systematic,
we don't even *try* to read all of them, held secure
in conviction of endless largesse.

                       Bet's glinting hair
in tendrils around her face. Her hands
thin. A spirit
woven of silk, has grown in her, as if bodily strength,
dwindling, had been a cocoon,
                    and only by this strange weakness
could her intelligence be freed, that instructs
the poet in me.
Alone at home, in between visits, I write, paint,
read and read, practice *Für Elise* with feeling
                         (and too much pedal)
help with the housework or shirk it,
and wait.

What did he say to us, Chekhov? Who was this Chekhov
pacing the round of the Whitestone Pond,
his hand on the chair coming down Heath Street,
telling the tale of Kashtanka in the gloomy sickroom
back at Heath Mansions?
                                        Ah, even though
the dark gauze of youth
swaddled us,
                    while airraids and news of battle
were part of each ominous day, and in flashes of dread
we glimpsed invasion, England and Europe gone down
utterly into the nightmare;
                                        even though Bet
was fading, month by month, and no one knew why–
we were open to life and hope: it was that he gave us,
generous, precise, lifting us
into the veins of a green leaf, translucent,
setting our hearts' tinder alight,
                                        sun striking on glass to release
the latent flames.

When the Black Monk
swiftly drew near, a whirlwind column grown
                                        from a pinpoint
to giant size, then–shrinking to human measure,
and passing inaudibly–moved through the solid trees
to vanish like smoke,
                            we thrilled to the presence of a power,
unquestioning. We knew
everything and nothing, nothing and everything.
Glimpsing a verity we could not define,
we saw that the story is not about illusion,
it's about what is true: 'the great garden
        with its miraculous flowers,
        the pines with their shaggy roots,
        the ryefield, marvellous science, youth,
        daring, joy . . .' That was the Chekhov we knew.

And the betrothed girl, who listens and listens
to a different and useful life calling her, and *does*

wrench herself free and go to study–and more,
comes back and *again* frees herself, journeying forth
(because a man dying, who himself
could not be free, gave her
his vision) into the hard, proto-revolutionary future,
her step forward for all of us,
as his words were for her–she was the Chekhov
who slipped unrecognized into our dreaming days.
She was at Bet's side when Bet,
a woman with grown children, so changed
from the girl in the wheelchair, a woman alone
with years of struggle behind her, sturdy–
yet still afraid–began, in spite of her fear,
to learn to teach. And at *my* side
in Berkeley, Boston, Washington, when we held our line
before advancing troopers, or sang out, 'Walk,
don't run,' retreating from gas and billyclubs,

                                        trying to learn
to act in the world.
                     She, The Betrothed,
whose marriage was not with her fiancé but with her life's
need to grow, to work for Chekhov's
    'Holy of holies–the human body, health, intelligence,
    inspiration, love,
    and the most absolute
    freedom from violence and lying'–she
was the Chekhov we knew.

                     What he would mean to us
we still can know only in part. (What has the Heath,
which Bet has lived close to always, and I,
through decades away, never quite lost sight of,
meant in our lives? A place of origin
gives and gives, as we return to it,
bringing our needs.) What he has meant
and goes on meaning, can't be trapped
into closed definition. But it has to do
not with failure, defeat, frustration,
Moscows never set out for,

but with love.
                    The sharp steel
of his scorn for meanness and cruelty gleamed
over our sheltered heads only half-noticed,
and irony was beyond our grasp,
we couldn't laugh with him; nevertheless
some inkling of rectitude and compassion
came to us, breathed in
under the fragrant leaves in wartime London, to endure
somewhere throughout the tumult of years. How,
                                    in our crude,
vague, dreamy ignorance could we recognize
              'the subtle, elusive beauty of human grief'?
Yet from between the dark green bindings
it rose, wafting into us, ready
to bide its time. The man who imagined a ring
inscribed with the words, 'Nothing passes,'
that rich man's son whom the townsfolk called
                                    'Small Gain,'
who suffered loss after loss, and was
                                    'left with the past,'
he too—for beyond despair
he carried in him the seed of change, the vision,
seeing not only *what is* but *what might be*—
he too was the Chekhov we knew, unknowing.

                              As we looked out
into the haze from that open height
familiar to Keats and Constable in their day—
a place built not only of earth but of layers
of human response, little hill
in time, in history—
your smile, Chekhov, 'tender, delightful, ironic,'
looked over our shoulders; and still looks, now,
half of our lifetime gone by, or more,
till we turn to see
who you were, who you are, everpresent, vivid,
luminous dust.

A Woman Meets an Old Lover

'He with whom I ran hand in hand
kicking the leathery leaves down Oak Hill Path
thirty years ago,

appeared before me with anxious face, pale,
almost unrecognized, hesitant,
lame.

He whom I cannot remember hearing laugh out loud
but see in mind's eye smiling, self-approving,
wept on my shoulder.

He who seemed always
to take and not give, who took me
so long to forget,

remembered everything I had so long forgotten.'

A Woman Alone

When she cannot be sure
which of two lovers it was with whom she felt
this or that moment of pleasure, of something fiery
streaking from head to heels, the way the white
flame of a cascade streaks a mountainside
seen from a car across a valley, the car
changing gear, skirting a precipice,
climbing . . .
When she can sit or walk for hours after a movie
talking earnestly and with bursts of laughter
with friends, without worrying
that it's late, dinner at midnight, her time
spent without counting the change . . .

90

When half her bed is covered with books
and no one is kept awake by the reading light
and she disconnects the phone, to sleep till noon . . .
Then
selfpity dries up, a joy
untainted by guilt lifts her.
She has fears, but not about loneliness;
fears about how to deal with the aging
of her body—how to deal
with photographs and the mirror. She feels
so much younger and more beautiful
than she looks. At her happiest
—or even in the midst of
some less than joyful hour, sweating
patiently through a heatwave in the city
or hearing the sparrows at daybreak, dully gray,
toneless, the sound of fatigue—
a kind of sober euphoria makes her believe
in her future as an old woman, a wanderer,
seamed and brown,
little luxuries of the middle of life all gone,
watching cities and rivers, people and mountains,
without being watched; not grim nor sad,
an old winedrinking woman, who knows
the old roads, grass-grown, and laughs to herself . . .
She knows it can't be:
that's Mrs. Doasyouwouldbedoneby from
                                  The Water-Babies,

no one can walk the world any more,
a world of fumes and decibels.
But she thinks maybe
she could get to be tough and wise, some way,
anyway. Now at least
she is past the time of mourning,
now she can say without shame or deceit,
O blessed Solitude.

He is scared of the frankness of women
which attracts and, when he draws near to listen,
may repulse or ignore him. This morning
in lazy sunlight's veil of clear and pale honey
poured from the sky's blue spoon,
they were laughing, talking over coffee about
misadventures, lovers, their own bodies,
and didn't stop when he came to join them, stepping
from indoor shade onto the charmed
and dappled stone ground of their terrace.

If any one of them had been
alone there, surely
his presence would have changed her,
he'd have seen that flicker, the putting aside
of her solitude to make room for him?
Together they seem almost blind to him.

Later, when they have gone to see bubbles of glass
blown into phantasmagoric precisions,
he takes a gondola, sliding past the palazzos,
and counts bridges. It's not (he thinks to himself
at some dark place in his mind, an intersection
of narrow seldom-navigated canals) that I want
their entire attention: that would demand–oh,
a response
nothing assures me I can give.
It's that when I see
their creature freedom, the way they can
fling themselves into the day!–as I,
being a strong swimmer, fling myself sometimes
into the ocean off a sailboat:
then I envy them.

If they had stopped (he wonders)
when I came out to their table,

interrupted themselves to acknowledge me alien,
would I have felt more excluded or less?
Their frankness, their uninterrupted friendship,
the sunlight lacing their hair, their
bright clothes, the three of them, their eyes
friendly but without mercy, without
the mercy of distance . . . When they
admit me, passing the creamjug,
to their laughter, laughter and even
    the confession of their own
troubles, about which they speak
so simply, so freely,
I am afraid.

The gondola shoots back out
as if with a sighing triumph into the breadth
and glitter of the Grand Canal,
the golden façades, vaporetti bustling,
pigeons wheeling up from the piazza.
He pays the silent gondolier, to whom
he has nothing to say, no way
to convince him he is a person,
and lands, to stroll
back to the hotel, back to wait
till the women return,
drawn by what he fears.

Fellow Passengers

A handsome fullgrown child, he seems,
in his well-chosen suit and wedding-ring,
hair not too long or short, taking
a business trip, surely one of his first—

listening enthralled to the not-much-older
bearded man in the window seat,

a returned mercenary, bragging of Africa:
bronzed, blondish, imperial pirate
half audible, thrillingly, under the jet's monotonous
subdued growling.

The baby businessman, naïf, laughs, excitement
springing from him in little splashes–his aura
fragmented–at a whiff of
soiled romance. It is something morbid
that flutters his dark thick lashes, gestures
with such well-cared-for hands,

hands his young wife
must want to bite, when they fumble,
innocent and impatient,
at her tense thighs.

May 1976

A Mystery (Oaxaca, Mexico)

A gust of night rain lightly
sweeps the dusty *Zocalo,* and the moon is down.
Mariachis are wrapping soft old cloths
around their instruments, and laying them reverently
in dingy cases, the way peasant grandsons
wrap ancient grandmothers,
                              laying them back in their cribs.
The last tourists, watched by waiters whose features
are carved by obsidian knives to regard
bloodsacrifice, are on the move
under the *portales,* pushing back chairs,
draining a last *cerveza Moctezuma,* leaving
here a forgotten *US News,* there
                              a half-full pack of Luckies

some beer spilled on;
                         and the sound of their voices,
Texans, New Englanders, hippies from California,
all the same to him, nasal and familiar, dwindles
as they scatter to sleep or sex or cards
or whatever the *yanquis* do by night.
Decades he has passed
back and forth and around and back and forth
in this square; and always the weight
of many *serapes,* heavy, and in the sun, hot,
on his shoulder. Of course he makes sales,
he spreads out the topmost one so they can see
the whole design. Some ignore him, some
wave him away, some he knows and nods to sometimes,
                                              they come
year after year and no longer buy, but they once did or
                                          still might–
but always there are some new ones, eager,
                              easily impressed–yes,
he sells, he is not poor–no, looking around him
                              he can see that anyone
looking from him to the shoeshine men, even,
not to speak of the barefoot boys with trays of quivering
ruby and gold and emerald *gelatinas,*
or the women nursing their babies down in the dust,
                                              ignoring
the ceaseless buzzing of wasps that are drunk all day
on candied fruits that sell by the piece,
women who take home scarcely the price of supper–
anyone looking from them to him can see he's not poor,
as poor goes. He's in business,
that's how he likes to think of himself. But still
he keeps walking, leaning always a bit
to one side from the weight.
                         He can't remember
his boyhood well. When he was young there was
                              something he wanted badly,
some desire that flamed in his eyes once,

like a spiralling saint's-day star it was,
rising from the heart when someone, something,
put a match to it . . . What was it? He's calm, but
                                        there's something
he can't remember.

The *tejedoras*, weavers,
Trixe women from the mountains, who all day
sit at work in the *Alameda* under the trees,
have gone with their little looms, their children,
                                        the two or three men
who come down from their villages with them,
                                        gone for the night
to sleep wherever they sleep.
The dome of the bandstand gleams, rainsprinkled, lit
by the tall street-lamps whose light
is somehow more silent and steady than darkness.
Here and there, now, one can see a few grayish figures
that have not left for the night's rest
but have begun to take it, tucked
as best they can into the angle of wall and sidewalk
or, if they dare, in a doorway,
some drunk, some homeless, all, certainly
of a poverty he has no truck with. Still,
he keeps walking. The bells of two unsynchronized
clocks are ringing:–eleven–midnight. A dog's howling
down by the market somewhere. The chairs and tables
from the cafés on three sides of the *Zocalo*
have been taken in or stacked–the fourth side,
floodlit, elegant, menacing, guarded always, is The Police,
The Government–a palace.
                                        There's no-one
to whom to open the topmost *serape*,
outshaking its firm folds, to display
a god, a bird, a geometry some say
has some intention. No one to speak to. '*Este jardin
es suyo. Cuidelo,*' say the signs among grass and flowers;
deterrent branches of thorns have been strewn on the
                                        neat parterres.

                                        A stranger,
crossing the *Zocalo* at a distance, solitary, glances his way.
He doesn't know that the stranger thinks,
'Doesn't the old man ever long
simply to put down his weight of woven wool
and lie down? Lie down and rest?
Here, anywhere, now,
and be still? He's been carrying through the years
a nest of blankets, a bed–heavier
than I can imagine . . . If that temptation were mine,
what could keep me walking, walking,
always carrying my wares? I'd lie down
as if in the snow . . .'

The 90th Year

for Lore Segal

High in the jacaranda shines the gilded thread
of a small bird's curlicue of song–too high
for her to see or hear.
                    I've learned
not to say, these last years,
'O, look!–O, listen, Mother!'
as I used to.

                    (It was she
who taught me to look;
to name the flowers when I was still close to the ground,
my face level with theirs;
or to watch the sublime metamorphoses
unfold and unfold
over the walled back gardens of our street . . .

It had not been given her
to know the flesh as good in itself,

as the flesh of a fruit is good. To her
the human body has been a husk,
a shell in which souls were prisoned.
Yet, from within it, with how much gazing
her life has paid tribute to the world's body!
How tears of pleasure
would choke her, when a perfect voice,
deep or high, clove to its note unfaltering!)

She has swept the crackling seedpods,
the litter of mauve blossoms, off the cement path,
tipped them into the rubbish bucket.
She's made her bed, washed up the breakfast dishes,
wiped the hotplate. I've taken the butter and milkjug
back to the fridge next door–but it's not my place,
visiting here, to usurp the tasks
that weave the day's pattern.
Now she is leaning forward in her chair,
          by the lamp lit in the daylight,
rereading *War and Peace*.
                    When I look up
from her wellworn copy of *The Divine Milieu,*
which she wants me to read, I see her hand
loose on the black stem of the magnifying glass,
she is dozing.
'I am so tired,' she has written to me, 'of appreciating
the gift of life.'

A Daughter (I)

When she was in the strangers' house–
      good strangers, almost relatives, good house,
      so familiar, known for twenty years,
      its every sound at once, and without thought,
      interpreted:
                but alien, deeply alien–

when she was there last week, part of her wanted
only to leave. It said, *I must escape*–no,
crudely, in the vernacular: *I gotta get outta here,*
it said.

And part of her
ached for her mother's pain,
her dying here–at home, yet far away from home,
thousands of miles of earth and sea, and ninety years
from her roots. The daughter's one happiness
during the brief visit that might be her last
(no, last but one: of course there would always be
what had stood for years at the end of some highway of
factual knowledge, a terminal wall;
there would be words to deal with: funeral, burial,
                                        disposal of effects;
the books to pack up)–her one happiness *this* time
was to water her mother's treasured, fenced-in garden,
a Welsh oasis where she remembers adobe rubble
two decades ago. Will her mother now
ever rise from bed, walk out of her room,
                                see if her yellow rose
has bloomed again?
Rainbows, the dark earthfragrance, the whisper of
                                        arched spray:
the pleasure goes back
to the London garden, forty, fifty years ago,
her mother younger than *she* is now.
And back in the north, watering the blue ajuga
                        (far from beginnings too, but it's a place
                        she's chosen as home)
the daughter knows
another, hidden part of her longed–or longs–
for her mother to be her mother again,
consoling, judging, forgiving,
whose arms were once
                        strong to hold her and rock her,
who used to chant
                        a ritual song that did magic

to take away hurt. Now mother is child, helpless; her mind
is clear, her spirit proud, she can even laugh–
but half-blind, half-deaf, and struck down
in body, she's a child in being at the mercy
of looming figures who have the power
to move her, feed her, wash her, leave or stay
at will. And the daughter feels, with horror,
metamorphosed: *she's* such a looming figure–huge–a

                                  tower

of iron and ice–love
shrunken in her to a cube of pain
locked in her throat. O, long and long ago
she grew up and went
away and away–and now's bereft
of tears and unable
to comfort the child her mother's become.
Instead, by the bedside, briskly, nervously,
carries out doctor's orders;
                  or travelling endlessly
in the air-conditioned sameness of jet-plane efficiency,
withdraws into lonely distance
(the patient left in the best of hands).

Watering the blue ajuga in her Boston yard
she imagines her mother may, after all,
be needing her–should she have left?
Imagines her mother at six years old in the riverfield,
twelve years old in her orphan's mourning,
twenty, forty, eighty–the storied screen unfolding,
told and told–and the days untold. A life!
A life–ninetythree years unique in the aeons.
She wants to go back to Mexico, sit by her mother,
have her be strong and say, *Go, child, and I bless you.*
She did say it! But weakly; it wasn't enough; she wants
to hear it again and again.

                  But she does not go back. Remembers
herself as a monstrous, tall, swift-moving nurse.
And remembers the way

she longed to leave, while she was there,
trapped in the house of strangers.
Something within her twists and turns,
she is tired and ashamed. She sobs, but her eyes
cannot make tears. She imagines herself
entering a dark cathedral to pray, and blessedly
falling asleep there, and not wakening
for a year, for seven years, for a century.

A Daughter (II)

Heading south, above
thick golden surf of cloud.
Along the western earthcurve,
eternal sunset, a gaunt red,
crouches, a wing outstretched,
immobile.
        Southward, deathward, time inside the jet
pauses. A drone of deafness–'Would you care
to purchase a cocktail?' mouthed
ritually. She clings, drink in hand,
to her isolation.

        A day later begins
the witnessing. A last week of the dying.
When she inserts
        quivering spoonfuls of violently
green or red *gelatina*
        into the poor obedient mouth,
she knows it's futile. Hour by hour
the body that bore her
shrinks and grows colder
and suffers. But days go by, and the long nights.

Each dawn the daughter, shivering,
opens the curtained door

and steps out on the balcony; and from time to time
leans there during the days. Mornings,
emphatic sunlight seizes the bougainvillea's
dry magenta blossoms. Among sharp stones, below,
of the hospital patio,
                              an ugly litter of cigarette stubs
thrown down by visitors leaning, anxious or bored,
from other balconies. No one sweeps up.
Sobs shake her–no tears. She hates
the uncaring light.

                    Afternoons
it's better, when impetuously
the rain hurls itself earthward for an hour.
Abruptly it stops, the steep streets
are full of the voice of rivers, adobe-brown,
sky still dark for a while.

Mostly, when there's no help to be given the nurse,
no feeding, moving, changing of sheets to be done,
and vital signs have been checked once more,
she sits with her back to the light
and listens–eyes on whatever book her mind
hungrily moves in, making its way
alone, holding on–listens
to hiss of oxygen and the breathing,
still steady,
she knows will
change rhythm, change
again,
and stop.

            Some force roaming the universe,
malicious and stupid, affixed, she feels,
this postscript to so vivid a life.
This tide that does not ebb, this persistence
stuck like a plane in mournful clouds,
what can it signify?
                              is any vision

102

–an entrance into a garden
of recognitions and revelations, Eden
of radiant comprehensions, taking
timeless place in the wounded head, behind
the closed, or glazed half-open, eyes?
Are words of deserved joy
singing behind the sunken lips that bent
stiffly into a formal smile when the daughter arrived again,
but now shape only *no* when pain
forces them back to speech?

There are flies in the room. The daughter
busies herself, placing wet gauze
over her mother's mouth and eyes.
                              What she wants
she knows she can't have: one minute
of communion, here in limbo.
                              All the years of it,
talk, laughter, letters. Yet something
went unsaid. And there's no place
to put whatever it was, now,
no more chance.

Death in Mexico

Even two weeks after her fall,
three weeks before she died, the garden
began to vanish. The rickety fence gave way
as it had threatened, and the children threw
broken plastic toys–vicious yellow,
unresonant red, onto the path, into the lemontree;
or trotted in through the gap, trampling small plants.
For two weeks no one watered it, except
I did, twice, but then I left. She was still conscious then
and thanked me. I begged the others to water it–
but the rains began; when I got back there were violent,

sudden, battering downpours each afternoon.
                                        Weeds flourished,
dry topsoil was washed away swiftly
into the drains. Oh, there was green, still,
but the garden was disappearing–each day
less sign of the ordered,
thought-out oasis, a squared circle her mind
constructed for rose and lily, begonia
and rosemary-for-remembrance.
Twenty years in the making–
less than a month to undo itself;
and those who had seen it grow,
living around it those decades,
did nothing to hold it. Oh, Alberto did,
one day, patch up the fence a bit,
when I told him a future tenant would value
having a garden. But no one believed
the garden-maker would live (I least of all),
so her pain if she were to see the ruin
remained abstract, an incomprehensible concept,
impelling no action. When they carried her past
                                        on a stretcher,
on her way to the *sanatorio*, failing sight
transformed itself into a mercy: certainly
she could have seen no more than a greenish blur.
But to me the weeds, the flowerless rosebushes, broken
stems of the canna lilies and amaryllis, all
a lusterless jungle green, presented–
even before her dying was over–
an obdurate, blind, all-seeing gaze:
I had seen it before, in the museums,
in stone masks of the gods and victims.
A gaze that admits no tenderness; if it smiles, it
only smiles with sublime bitterness–no,
not even bitter: it admits
no regret, nostalgia has no part in its cosmos,
bitterness is irrelevant.
If it holds a flower–and it does,
a delicate brilliant silky flower that blooms only
a single day–it holds it clenched

between sharp teeth.
Vines may crawl, and scorpions, over its face,
but though the centuries blunt
eyelid and flared nostril, the stone gaze
is utterly still, fixed, absolute,
smirk of denial facing eternity.
Gardens vanish. She was an alien here,
as I am. Her death
was not Mexico's business. The garden though
was a hostage. Old gods
took back their own.

A Visit

i

Milk to be boiled
egg to be poached
pot to be scoured.

Bandage to bind
firm around old bones
cracked in a fall:

White hair to be brushed
cold feet to be warmed
gnarled toenails to cut.

When there is work to be done
moonwavering images
of sentiment and desire
ride away into the forest

and sexual songs
shake their preened wings
and fly off, casting
a few loose feathers

scarlet and purple

soon invisible.

ii

Over the mountains
lean the clouds
as if their shadows were mirrors.

Lay down poison
in the track of the ants
who devour the roses.

When there is work to do
one laughs at oneself,
the intense life of the heart
stops talking.

How frail, how small,
the body that bore me.
She too
is laughing:

'Skin and bones' she says.
'The bandage is like
a knight's armour,' she says.
'What dragons
are to be vanquished?'

Death Psalm: O Lord of Mysteries

She grew old.
She made ready to die.
She gave counsel to women and men, to young girls and
                                                    young boys.
She remembered her griefs.
She remembered her happinesses.
She watered the garden.
She accused herself.
She forgave herself.
She learned new fragments of wisdom.
She forgot old fragments of wisdom.
She abandoned certain angers.
She gave away gold and precious stones.
She counted-over her handkerchiefs of fine lawn.

She continued to laugh on some days, to cry on others,
                    unfolding the design of her identity.
She practiced the songs she knew, her voice
                              gone out of tune
                    but the breathing-pattern perfected.
She told her sons and daughters she was ready.
She maintained her readiness.
She grew very old.
She watched the generations increase.
She watched the passing of seasons and years.
She did not die.

She did not die but lies half-speechless, incontinent,
                    aching in body, wandering in mind
                    in a hospital room.
A plastic tube, taped to her nose,
        disappears into one nostril.
Plastic tubes are attached to veins in her arms.
Her urine runs through a tube into a bottle under the bed.
On her back and ankles are black sores.
The black sores are parts of her that have died.
The beat of her heart is steady.
She is not whole.

She made ready to die, she prayed, she made her peace,
        she read daily from the lectionary.
She tended the green garden she had made,
        she fought off the destroying ants,
        she watered the plants daily
        and took note of their blossoming.
She gave sustenance to the needy.
She prepared her life for the hour of death.
But the hour has passed and she has not died.

O Lord of mysteries, how beautiful is sudden death
        when the spirit vanishes
        boldly and without casting
        a single shadowy feather of hesitation
        onto the felled body.

108

O Lord of mysteries, how baffling, how clueless
   is laggard death, disregarding
   all that is set before it
      in the dignity of welcome—
   laggard death, that steals
      insignificant patches of flesh—
   laggard death, that shuffles
   past the open gate,
   past the open hand,
   past the open,
            ancient,
            courteously waiting life.

                                                A Soul-Cake

Mother, when I open a book of yours
your study notes fall out into my lap.
'Apse, semicircular or polygonal recess
arched over domed roof,' says one. I remember
your ceiling, cracked by earthquake,
and left that way. Not that you chose to leave it;
nevertheless, 'There's nothing less real
than the present,' you underlined.

My throat clenches when I weep and
can't make tears,
the way my feet clenched when I ran
unsuspecting into icy ocean
for 'General swim,' visiting Nik at summercamp.
What hurts is not your absence only,
dull, unresonant, final,
it's the intimate knowledge of your aspirations,
the scholar in you, the artist reaching
out and out.
            To strangers your unremitting
struggle to learn appears

a triumph–to me, poignant. I know
how baffled you felt.
I know only I
knew how lonely you were.
The small orphan,
skinny, proud, reserved, observant,
irreverent still in the woman of ninety,
but humble.

"To force conscience," you marked in Panofsky,
"is worse,' says Castellio, 'than cruelly
to kill a man. For to deny one's convictions
destroys the soul."
                    And Bruno's lines,
"The age
Which I have lived, live, and shall live,
Sets me atremble, shakes, and braces me."

Five months before you died you recalled
counting-rhymes, dance-games for me;
gaily, under the moon, you sang and mimed,

                  My shoes are very *dir*ty,
                  My shoes are very *thin,*
                  I haven't got a *pock*et
                  To put a penny in.

                  A soul-cake, a soul-cake,
                  Please, good missis, a soul-cake . . .

But by then for two years
you had hardly been able to hear me,
could barely see to read.
                    We spoke together
                    less and less.

There's too much grief. Mother,
what shall I do with it?
Salt grinding and grinding from the magic box.

110

Talking to Grief

Ah, grief, I should not treat you
like a homeless dog
who comes to the back door
for a crust, for a meatless bone.
I should trust you.

I should coax you
into the house and give you
your own corner,
a worn mat to lie on,
your own water dish.

You think I don't know you've been living
under my porch.
You long for your real place to be readied
before winter comes. You need
your name,
your collar and tag. You need
the right to warn off intruders,
to consider
my house your own
and me your person
and yourself
my own dog.

Earliest Spring

Iron scallops border the path, barely
above the earth; a purplish starling lustre.

Earth a different dark, scumbled, bare
between clumps of wintered-over stems.

Slowly, from French windows opened
to first, mild, pale, after-winter morning,
we inch forward, looking: pausing, examining
each plant. It's boring. The dry stalks
are tall as I, up to her thigh. But then–
'Ah! Look! A snowdrop!' she cries,
satisfied, and I see

thin sharp green darning-needles
stitch through the sticky gleam of dirt,

belled with white!
                    'And another!
And here, look, and here.'
                            A white carillon.
Then she stoops to show me precise
bright green check-marks

vivid on inner petals,
each outer petal
filing down to a point.

                    And more:
'Crocuses–yes, here they are . . .'

and these point upward, closed
tight as eyelids waiting a surprise,

egg-yoke gold or mauve;
and she brings my gaze

to filigree veins of violet
traced upon white, that make

the mauve seem. This is the earliest
spring of my life. Last year

I was a baby, and what I saw then
is forgotten. Now I'm a child. Now I'm not bored

at moving step by step,
slow, down the path. Each pause

brings us to bells or flames.

Emblem (I)

Dreaming, I rush
thrust from the cave of the winds,
into the midst of a wood of tasks.
The boughs part, I sweep
poems and people with me a little way;
dry twigs, small patches of earth
are cleared and covered.
Then I find myself
out over open heath, a sigh that holds
a single note, heading
far and far to the horizon's bent firtree.

Emblem (II)

A silver quivering cocoon that shakes
from within, trying to break.
                              What psyche
is wrestling with its shroud?
Blunt diamonds
scrape at its casing,
urging it out.
But there is too much grief. The world
is made of days, and is itself
a shrouded day.
It stifles. It's our world, and we
its dreams, its creased
compacted wings.

113

Kindness

'Was it eyes of friendship the dog had?'
Robert Duncan, 1964, writing about
a poem, 'As It Happens.'

Eyes of kindness that the dog had,
the 3-legged beggar dog,
were not eyes of friendship–no:
in its hunger, dog
gave over to the stricken
heart of a watcher–not a giver–
(bereaved, an alien
for a time among the living)
agony. Shared it. As that watcher
would share a used-up bone, a crust.
In a fog of dust and grief
in the sun
the dog's hurt life
was itself
a kindness. Timidly
the beast took
the afterthought of bread.
The traveller took
in exchange
its gift
for a while, and
wept in it, enabled.

What a flimsy shred of the world
I hold by its tenuous, filmy edge!
All my multitudes,
the tribes of my years passing
        into murmurous caverns,
the grassblades, flinty paths,
words, baled reams of inscribed paper, cities,
cities recurring composite
in dream,
            skin, breath, lashes, hair,
closeups, perspectives–a hive of knowledge
no bigger than a bead of sweat.

Fish are uttering silence in the ocean's holes–
and all about me,
unconceived,
the foundries, steelmill flames aloft flaring, clangor,
the vast routine of power,
what it is to be threadbare,
breathe asbestos,
daily for fifty years to tread
certain adamantine steps,
                        kill, to have killed.

Unknown lurchings into calculus, landing
the plane I fly in. And each other dreamer
clutching (wideawake) a different frayed
scrap of fabric!
            Are there gods whose pleasure
is to make rag rugs, deftly
braiding? Quilts for eternity? Needled blood
from Chthonian fingers speckling
the ritual patterns?

Scornful Reprieve

Curtly the sky
plucks
at knots of cloud;
from the unfurled bundles
out roll pellets
of leaden rain,
singly, savagely,
dropping, to pock
the pale
          dust of the earth.
Something cannot believe
a gift has been given.
Shall grass indeed
grow here?

Alongside

Catbird cadenzas from the bushes
issue like edicts. See him! Fearless,
intent upon invention, slate blue
among the dewy leaves, his puffed throat
pumping. Alongside
the human day, his day,
fully engaged.
                    Miaow!
A bright glance registers
old Two-legs passing by. Not his concern,
pah! A billion leaves
demand utterance, he has the whole
hillside to sing, the veil of vapor.
Azaleas must be phrased! And dandelions—
a golden pizzicato!
Soon enough
it will be noon, and hot, and silent.

Run Aground

A brown oakleaf, left over from last year,
turns into a bird and flies off singing.

That should encourage you!   I know it–
but I'm not an oakleaf.

I'm not singing.

I'm not watching the brown wings
cleave the air.

The cold half-moon
sits obstinate in this warm, middle-of-the-day,
middle of the month.

I'm looking sullenly back at it,
human, thrown
back on my own resources.

Intimation

Some trick of light

in the reflection of sunny kitchen against
a dark wall in back of the yard

makes this morning's daffodils
that shout for joy, thronging their stone vase,
leaning outward in a ring,
golden, hilarious, ready for anything,
for spring–

makes them into a cluster
of yellow chrysanthemums,
no less beautiful,
                    but very still,
facing November,
facing frost.

Autumnal

Through the high leafy branches
rush of wind-flood.   Gleam
of the wind's teeth
at dead of night, *calavera.*
Dark of the moon.
Under the smiling skin
bloodstream furtively
slower.   The wind sweeping aside
the weir of leaves. Meshing
of counterrhythms. So,
is this how time
takes one? Bricks returned to clay
in Nineveh? Sheba's gazebo
silted over, under
the desert tides?

The Long Way Round

for Alice Walker and Carolyn Taylor

i

'The solution,' they said to my friend,
'lies in eventual total'–they said (or 'final'?),
'assimilation. Miscegeny. No more trouble–'
        Disappear, they said.

I in America,
       white, an
              indistinguishable mixture
of Kelt and Semite, grown under glass
in a British greenhouse, a happy
old-fashioned artist, sassy and free,

had to lean in yearning towards
the far-away daughters and sons of
Vietnamese struggle
before I could learn,
       begin to learn,
by Imagination's slow ferment,
what it is to awaken
each day Black in White America,
each day struggling
        to affirm
a who-I-am my white skin never
has to pay heed to.
        Who I am
slowly, slowly
        took lessons
from distant Asia; and only then
from near-as-my-hand persons, Black sisters.

Pushing open my mind's
door on its grating hinges
to let in the smell of
pain, of destroyed
flesh, to know
        for one instant's agony,
        insisted on for the sake of knowing
        anything, anything at all
        in truth,
that that flesh belonged
to one's own most dear,
child, or lover, or mother–

pushing open my door I began
to know who I was and
who I was not.
And slowly–for though
it's in a flash we
know we know,
yet before that flash there's a long
slow, dull, movement of fire
along the well-hidden
line of the fuse–

I came to know,
        in the alembic
of grief and will and love,
just barely to know, by knowing
it never
     ever
        would be what I could
know in the flesh,

what it must be to wake each day
to the sense of one's own beautiful
human skin, hair, eyes, one's
whole warm sleep-caressed body

as something that others
hated,
      hunted,
            haunted by its otherness,
something they wanted to see disappear.

iii

Swimming, we are, all of us, swimming
in the rectangular indoor claustrophobic pool
–echoing, sharply smelling of chlorine,
stinging our eyes–
that is
our life,

           where,
        scared and put off our stroke
        but righting ourselves with a gasp
           sometimes we touch
an Other,
        another
breathing and gasping body,
'yellow,' but not yellow at all,
'black,' but most often
brown; shaped like ourselves, bodies we could
embrace in relief, finding
ourselves not alone in the water.

         And someone,
           some fool of a coach,
strutting the pool's edge, wading
the shallow end, waves his arms at us,
shouting,
        'If you're White
        you have
        the right of way!'

While we
swim for dear life, all of us–'not,'
as it has been said, *'not* waving,
but drowning.'

On the 32nd Anniversary
of the Bombing of Hiroshima and Nagasaki*

A new bomb, big one, drops
a long way beyond the fence of our minds'
property. And they tell us, *'With this
the war is over.'*
                    We are twenty years old, thereabouts–
now stale uniforms
can fall off our backs, replaced
by silk of youth! Relief,
not awe, gasps from our
mouths and widens
ignorant eyes. We've been used
to the daily recitation of death's
multiplication tables: we don't notice
the quantum leap: eighty-seven thousand
killed outright by a single bomb,
fifty-one thousand missing or injured.
We were nurses, refugees, sailors, soldiers,
familiar with many guises of death: war had ended our
                                                 childhood.
We knew about craters, torpedoes, gas ovens.
This we ignored.
The rumor was distant traffic. Louder
were our heartbeats,
                    summer was springtime:
'The war is over!'

* See note on page 275.

And on the third day no-one
rose from the dead at Hiroshima,
and at Nagasaki
the exploit was repeated, as if
to insist we take notice:
seventy-three thousand
killed by one bomb,
seventy-four thousand injured or missing.
Familiar simple-arithmetic of
mortal flesh did not serve,
                              yet I cannot remember,
and Sid, Ruth, Betty, Matthew, Virginia
cannot remember August sixth or
August ninth, nineteen-
forty-five. *The war was over* was all we knew
and a vague wonder, *what next? What will ordinary
life be like, now ordinary life as we know it
is gone?*

But the shadow,
the human shadowgraph sinking itself
indelibly upon stone at Hiroshima
as a man, woman or child was consumed
in unearthly fire—
                    that shadow
already had been for three days
imprinted upon our lives.
Three decades now we have lived
with its fingers outstretched in horror clinging
to our future, our children's future,
into history or the void.
The shadow's voice
cries out to us to cry out.
Its nails dig
            into our souls
                            to wake them:
'*Something*,' it ceaselessly
repeats, its silence
a whisper, its whisper

a shriek,
      while 'the radiant gist'
is lost, and the moral labyrinths of
humankind convulse as if made
of snakes clustered and intertwined and stirring
from long sleep–
'. . . *something can yet*
be salvaged upon the earth:
try, try to survive,
try to redeem
the human vision
from cesspits where human hands
have thrown it, as I was thrown
from life into shadow. . . .'

For Chile, 1977

It was a land where the wingéd mind
could alight.
Andean silver dazzling the Southern Cross;
the long shore of gold beaten by the Pacific
into translucency, vanishing
into Antarctica–
      yes, these:
   but not for these
our minds flew there,

but because they knew
the poor were singing there
and the homeless
were building there
and the downtrodden
were dancing.

How brief it was, that time
when Chile showed us how to rejoice!

How soon the executioners
arrived, making victims
of those who were not born to be victims.

The throats of singers
were punched into silence,
hands of builders
crushed,
dancers herded
into the pens.

How few
all over the earth,
from pole to pole, are the lands
where our minds can perch and be glad,
clapping their wings, a phoenix flock!

From Chile now
they fly affrighted, evil smoke
rises from forest and city,
hopes are scorched.

When will the cheerful hammers sound again?
When will the wretched begin to dance again?
When will guitars again
give forth at the resurrected touch
of broken fingers
a song of revolution reborn?

Greeting to the Vietnamese Delegates to the U. N.

Our large hands
Your small hands

Our country's power
Our powerlessness against it

Your country's poverty
The power of your convictions

Our corrupted democracy
The integrity of your revolution

Our technology and its barbarity
Your ingenuity and simple solutions

Our bombers
Your bicycles

Our unemployed veterans
Your re-educated prostitutes

Our heroin addicts rotting
Your wounded children healing

Our longing for new life
Your building of new life

Our large hands
Your small hands

Some beetle trilling
its midnight utterance.

Voice of the scarabee,
dungroller,
working survivor . . .

I recall how each year
returning from voyages, flights
over sundown snowpeaks,
cities crouched over darkening lakes,
hamlets of wood and smoke,
I find
        the same blind face upturned to the light
        and singing
        the one song,

        the same weed managing
        its brood of minute stars
        in the cracked flagstone.

MODULATIONS FOR SOLO VOICE

These poems were written in the winter and spring of 1974–75, and might be subtitled, from the cheerful distance of 1978, *Historia de un amor.* They are intended to be read as a sequence.

> 'There are the lover and the beloved, but
> these two come from different countries.'
> Carson McCullers
> *The Ballad of the Sad Café*

From Afar

The world is round.
Amber beads
I took from around my neck
before we lay down, before
you left to go onward and homeward,
remind me, and the saying:
'Each place on earth is
the middle of the world.'

A certain blue would be
your color, no? Dark
as your irises
that ringed black tarns
I looked into,
             that looked
back at me,
gaze holding.

•

I could sail around the world looking
for your country
and never find it—what would it mean to me
unless you were in it,
it is you I want, to look
with love into me,
to come into me,
you who came out of the
bluest furthest distance.
Who left so soon, going
inexorably
north into snow,

        like a messenger gone into Lapland
        with runes for the watchful sages,
        with gentleness wrapped in linen to give
        their crystal princess
        under those stern auroras.

•

I wanted to learn you by heart.
There was only time
for the opening measures—a minor key,
major chords, arpeggios of desire that ripple
        swifter than I can hum them—
and through all
a lucid, dreaming tune
that gleaners sing
alone in the fields.

I am wayfaring
in the middle of the world,
treading water, the blue
of your absence,
cold ocean; trudging
the dusty earth-curves
to unending distance,
round and round.
Listening for that music,

singing within me
the first notes over,
as if in the middle of the
round world you could hear me?

Silk

i

Halfawake, I think
silky hair, cornsilk, his voice
of one substance with
his words, with
his warm flesh.
I put my hand out
in the dark to touch
his letter, placed
in reach for the night's
shoals of waking.
What I know of him
is a flow unbroken
from word to touch,
from body to thought's
dance or stillness.
Therefore into my palm
off the paper
rises what soothes me,
indivisible;
I can return
into the sea of sleep.

ii

Today the telephone
brought me his voice itself:
the silk of it
is darker than I remembered,
and warmer.
I took the folds of it up
to wrap myself in,
to keep off the cold of
all the snowfields between us.

The Phonecall°

Big bluejay black,
white sky in back; brittle;
twisting bare random
branches.   Morning
persists in rain, rain
that last night
dripped from the eaves
in pacing footsteps.
Awake and awake
I was ashamed:
only lonely private sorrows
took my sleep—
(*only lonely, only lonely* . . . as if a child
sat in a treehouse,
moping). Politics,
the word I use to mean
striving for justice and for
mercy, never
keeps me so long
open-eyed. The world's

° See note on page 275.

crowded with crowded
prisons; if Debs
was truthful, humankind
can feel more than
I know or
for more than a moment
can sustain. What turns
the jay blue
again in gray
rainlight is not,
this morning, news
of any justice or freedom
but (o infinitesimal,
fragile, vast, only!)
the mercy of one voice
speaking from far away
lowpitched, loving,
one to one . . .

Psyche in Somerville

I am angry with X, with Y, with Z,
for not being you.
Enthusiasms jump at me,
wagging and barking. Go away.
Go home.

I am angry with my eyes for not seeing you,
they smart and ache and see the snow,
an insistent brilliance.

If I were Psyche how could I not
bring the lamp to our bedside?
I would have known in advance
all the travails my gazing
would bring, more than Psyche

ever imagined,
and even so, how could I not have raised
the amber flame to see
the human person I knew
was to be revealed.
She did not even know! She dreaded
a beast and discovered
a god. But I
know, and hunger
to witness again the form
of mortal love itself.

I am angry with everything that is filling
the space of your absence,
breathing your air.
                    Psyche,
how blessed you were
in the dark, knowing him in your flesh:
I was wrong! If I were Psyche
I would live on in darkness, and endure
the foolish voices, barking of aeolian dogs,
                              the desert glitter
of days full of boring treasures,
walking on precious stones till my feet hurt,

to hold you each night and be held
close in your warmth in a pitchblack cave of a room

and not have to wait
for Mercury, dressed in the sad gray coat of a mailman
and no wings on his feet,
to bring me your words.

A Woman Pacing Her Room, Rereading a Letter, Returning Again and Again to Her Mirror

i

Poised on the edge of ugliness,

a flower whose petals
are turning brown.
                    I never liked
to keep them—a word of farewell
discreetly whispered, and out they go,
the discolored water after them,
the vase to be scrubbed.
                    A few flowers
dry into straw-crisp comeliness
without fetor. But
for most
            beauty is balanced upon
the poignance of brevity.

I have almost fallen already,
an ordinary flower.
But my lover talks about two years from now . . .
In two years I may be richly
gone into compost—juice and fiber
absorbed in the dark of
time past, my fever
a flame remembered,
                    old candle,
                    old shadow.
Or in two years I may be straw.

                    Flowers of straw,
everlastings, are winter makeshifts
pleasant to see, but not to touch.
Their voice is a faint crackling under the hand.

By spring the settled
        dust is dull
              upon brittleness,

        and someone brings in
posies of fragrance from the meadows,
violets, the forgotten, now-to-be-known-freshly
primrose;
        dew is on them,
        what could one ever
        desire but to sink with closed eyes
        into their cold, sweet, brief,
        silent music?

ii (The Woman Has Ceased to Pace, She Sits Down on the Edge of Her Bed, Still Holding the Letter)

We can't save
our tears in precious vials,
or if we do, we don't know
what to do with them then,
iridescent amphorae
        coated with salt . . .
                         We can't save
ourselves, I cannot hold
my fleeting, fading, ordinary hedgerow rays
                of sun or star homage
from falling, from leaving
        nothing but the small nub they flare from
–and that itself
swiftly or slowly must turn
from gold to mole-dark gray.

Dream: Château de Galais°

In dream you ask me
to care for your child while its mother
rides in the tapestry forest.
The whole château

is thronged with fair and strange
folk, both Frantz de Galais and his friends, and
your friends, my friends, and many
personages without whom my story
would have been a blank.

I lie down beside the child
to lull her to sleep, and I lull myself
to sleep. A remote attic, daytime, a room
where perhaps the godmother sometimes

                              sits at her spinning.

And when I awake, the belovéd
rosy and longlashed daughter, fragrant
with infant sweat, is curled
confidingly into my circling protective arm,
and you have entered the room

searching for me, for now at last
we can meet alone for an hour.
Smiling, your hand on the door, eager to leave.
It is a subtle and delicate task to rise
so softly she will not wake.
Tendrils of hair, silky like yours,
cling damp to my cheek
where her head nestles.
But you want me. You take my hands,

° See note on page 275.

we steal from the safe room quickly.
This was a dream
of sadness, of sleep, of a place
known to our minds, of seeking each other,
of joy.

Like Loving Chekhov

Loving this man who is far away
is like loving Anton Chekhov.
It is true, I do love Anton Chekhov,
I have loved him longer than I have known this man.
I love all the faces of Chekhov in my collection
of photos that show him in different years of his life,
alone, or with brothers and sisters, with actors,
                                      with Gorki,
with Tolstoi, with his wife, with his undistinguished
endearing pet dogs; from beardless student to pince-nez'd
famous and ailing man.
                          I have no photo
of the man I love.

I love Chekhov for travelling alone
to the prison island without being asked.
For writing of the boiling, freezing, terrible seas
around the island and around the lives of its people
that they 'resembled the scared dreams
of a small boy who's been reading
                          Lost in the Ocean Wastes
before going to sleep, and whose blanket has fallen off,
so he huddles shivering
and can't wake up.'
For treasuring the ugly inkstand a penniless seamstress
gave him in thanks for his doctoring.
If there's an afterlife,
I hope to meet Anton Chekhov there.

137

Loving the man I love
is like that, because he is far away,
and because he is scrupulous, and because surely
nothing he says or does can bore me.
But it's different too. Chekhov had died
long before I was born. This man is alive.
He is alive and not here.
This man has shared my bed, our bodies
have warmed each other and given each other
delight, our bodies
are getting angry with us for giving them to each other
                                      and then
allowing something they don't understand to
                                pry them apart,
                                a metallic
cruel wedge that they hear us call
necessity.
            Often it seems unreal to love
a man who is far away, or only real to the mind,
the mind teasing the body. But it's real,
he's alive, and it's not in the afterlife
I'm looking to see him,
but in this here and now, before I'm a month older,
before one more gray hair has grown on my head.
If he makes me think about Chekhov it's not because
he resembles him in the least but because the ache
of distance between me and a living man I know and
                                don't know
grips me with pain and fear, a pain and fear
familiar in the love of the unreachable dead.

'My delicate Ariel'–
can you imagine,
Caliban had a sister?
Not ugly, brutish, wracked with malice,
but nevertheless
earthbound half-sibling to him,
and, as you once were,
prisoned within a tree–
but that tree being
no cloven pine but the sturdy wood
her body seemed to her,
its inner rings revealing
slow growth,
its bark incised
with hearts and arrows,
all its leaves wanting to fly, and falling–
  and ever in spring again
   peering forth small as flint-sparks?

Spirit whose feet touch earth
only as spirit moves them,
imagine
   this rootbound woman,
Prospero's bastard daughter,
his untold secret, hidden from Miranda's
gentle wonder.
    Her intelligent eyes
watch you, her mind
can match your own, she loves
your grace of intellect.
But she knows
what weight of body is, knows her flesh
(her cells, her magic cell)
mutters its own dark songs.

                                    She loves
to see you pass by,
grieves that she cannot hold you,
knows it is so and *must* be;
offers the circle of her shade,
silvery Ariel,
for your brief rest.

                                        Modulations*

'The laws of modulation are found in *The Science of Harmony*,
       which treats of the formation and progression of chords.'
           Simple & Complete Primer for the Pianoforte, 1885

i

Easily we are happy, I was thinking, no need
for so much grieving,
ashen mind, heart flaming, flaming
from core of stone.

Easy days, nights when our bodies
were learning each other.

ii

But that perfection, nectarine of light—
you bruised it.
Impeccably conscientious,
gave it a testing pinch,

      * See note on page 275.

reminding me of my status
in the country of your affections:
secondclass citizen.

Don't you know I hate to be told
what I know already?
Remember the custodian telling us,
'This chair is beautiful,
this is a beautiful table'?
What I knew I'd taken already
on terms of my own:
not as defeat but with new freedom—
        from false pride,
        from measuring my value to you
        in a jeweller's finicky scale.

(And *the heart's affections* are *holy,*
we have known that, but have loved
to hear it again for the sake of
his life who said it. And *what the Imagination seizes
as beauty must be truth*—
yet there are hierarchies within that truth.)

iii

Nectarine of our pleasure,
enclosed in its own fragrance,
poised on its imaginary branch!
I imagine too quickly, giving to tenuous things
hasty solidity,
to irresolute shadows
a perfect equilibrium.

For you, then,
our days and nights had not been a river
flowing at leisure between grassy banks?

141

You thought I would try
to force the river
out of its course?

You didn't trust me . . .

iv

Or perhaps indeed
we did after all
share our pleasure,
halving the nectarine–

but even as we drifted
downstream at ease
and golden juices
stained your mind's tongue,

Anxiety arrived from your hometown
wearing black,
waving her umbrella?

v

Since I must recover
my balance, I do. I falter
but don't fall; recalling
how every vase, cut sapphire, absolute
dark rose, is not indeed
of rarest, of most cherished
perfection unless flawed,
offcentered, pressed
with rough thumbprint, bladescratch, brown
birthmark that tells
of concealed struggle from bud to open ease
of petals, soon
to loosen, to drop and
be blown away.

The asymmetrical
tree of life, fractionally lopsided
at the trunk's live-center
tells where a glancing eye,
        not a ruler,
drew, and drew strength
from its mistake.

The picture of perfection
must be revised.
Allow for our imperfections,
welcome them,
consume them into its substance.
Bring from necessity
its paradoxical virtue,
mortal life, that makes it
give off so strange a magnetic
shining, when one had thought
darkness had filled the night.

vi

These questions
that have walked beside all that I say,
waiting their turn for utterance:

        How do I free myself
        from pain self-imposed,

                pride-pain,
                will-pain,

                pain of wanting
                never to feel superfluous?

        How are you acted on
        by anxiety, by a coldness
        taught to you as a boy?

–these questions
are not mine only.
The vision

of river, of nectarine,

is not mine only.
All humankind,

women and men,

hungry,

hungry beyond the hunger
for food, for justice,

pick themselves up and stumble on
for this: to transcend barriers, longing

for absolution of each by each,
luxurious unlearning
of lies and fears,

for joy, that *throws down the reins*
on the neck of
                    the divine animal
who carries us through the world.

'Elle est Débrouillarde'

High on vitamins, I demonstrate to my friends
the *lezginka, mazurka, gavotte.* With a
one two three, hop, one two three, hop, teach
someone the polka.
                    Laughter's a joy
even next day at breakfast.

Do I really suffer
that his letters arrive so seldom—
unwritten or unmailed?
Is it love or pride that hurts?
Am I maybe
fully as jocund as I seem?

(Only twice I've cried
in weeks now—once
writing of my mother's
extreme old age, the slow
race between heart and sight;
once when I read about Li-li's
lost first love, when her parents
pulled her away to Taiwan,
away from her comrades.
Did they die in the struggle against Chiang Kai-shek?)

Is 'the fine art of unhappiness' truly
losing its allure?

From Afar (II)

The first poem
becomes the last.

The world
is round.
I am wayfaring.

I learned
the tense and slender
warmth of your body
almost by heart.

The bluest, furthest distance
is what you carry
within you—
the cold of it
inexorable.

I know
you can't hear me.

I'm gleaning
alone in a field
in the middle of the world,

you're listening
for a song that
I don't know,

that no one
yet has sung.

This is not
farewell.
I have
your word for it,
inviolate.
The last poem

enclosed in the lucid
amber of the world

becomes the first.

Epilogue

I thought I had found a swan
but it was a migrating snow-goose.

I thought I was linked invisibly to another's life
but I found myself more alone with him than without him.

I thought I had found a fire
but it was the play of light on bright stones.

I thought I was wounded to the core
but I was only bruised.

The Blue Rim of Memory

The way sorrow enters the bone
is with stabs and hoverings.
From a torn page
a cabriolet
approaches over the crest of a hill,
first the nodding, straining head of the horse
then the blind lamps, peering;

the ladies within the insect eagerly
look from side to side awaiting the vista–
and quick as a knife
are vanished. Who were they? Where is the hill?

Or from stoked fires of nevermore
a warmth constant as breathing hovers out
to surround you, a cloud of mist
becomes rain, becomes cloak, then skin.

The way sorrow enters the bone
is the way fish sink through dense lakes
raising smoke from the depth
and flashing sideways in bevelled
syncopations.
It's the way the snow
drains the light from day but then,
covering boundaries of road and sidewalk,
widens wondering streets
and stains the sky yellow
to glow at midnight.

Listen: the wind in new leaves
whispers, smoother than fingertips,
than floss silk smoothing through fingertips . . .

When the sighted
talk about *white* they may mean
silence of sullen cold, that winter–
no matter how warm your rooms
–waits with at the door.
(Though there's another whiteness,
more like the weightlessness of a flake of snow,
of a petal, a pine-needle . . .)

When they say *black* they may mean the persistence
of cold wind hopelessly, angrily,
tearing and tearing through leafless boughs.
(Though there's another blackness,
round and full as the notes of cello and drum . . .)

But this:
this lively, delicate shiver
that whispers itself caressingly
over our flesh
when leaves are moist and small
and winds are gentle,
is green. Light green. Not weightless,
light.

The Emissary

Twice now this woman for whom my unreasonable dislike
has slowly turned to loathing
has come up to me and said, 'Ah, yes,
we shall have plenty of time soon to talk.'

Twice she has laid her cold hand heavily
on mine,
and thrust her pallid face, her puffy cheeks,
close to mine.
I went to wash in the hottest water, to oil myself
in fragrant oils.

I know who she is in the world; others know her;
many seem not to notice she brings
a chill into rooms.
She is who she is,
ordinary, venal, perhaps sad.
Perhaps she is not aware of her own task:
but death sends her about the world.

I have always been afraid of pain
but not of death.
I am not afraid of death, but I don't want
to have time
to sit and talk with this woman.

I have watched her condescend
to those who don't know her name,
and smirk at the ones who do.
I have seen her signature
hiding under pebbles,
scratched into chips of ice.

She can have nothing to tell me
I could be glad to hear.
Twice she has looked at me

with eyes that gleam dull, a pewter gray.
Twice she has looked at me with a look
that gives me nothing I shall ever want.

Death is for everyone. I shall never willingly
give her the right to bring me my share.
I shall refuse to take what is mine
from her gray hands.

A Look at the Night (Temple, Early '60's)

The plough
the only constellation we are
sure of

turning
the sky's earth, faithful
among its furrows of wind–

And the fierce moon
a barn-owl, over
boughs and
bright clouds–

No one

> will speak for us
> no one
> but ourselves knows
> what our lives
> are.
> We step outdoors at
> 2 a.m., our minds
> dilated by deep
> early sleep,
to the quick of

           brilliant night
alone:
such words as
carry our testimony
                    singular,
                    incontrovertible,
                    breath and tongue awaiting
                    patent,
or do without.

We sing
in mutterings
to speak for ourselves.
           The turned field
black above us,
                    the moon
high in her dominion.

Wedding-Ring

My wedding-ring lies in a basket
as if at the bottom of a well.
Nothing will come to fish it back up
and onto my finger again.
                    It lies
among keys to abandoned houses,
nails waiting to be needed and hammered
into some wall,
telephone numbers with no names attached,
idle paperclips.
           It can't be given away
for fear of bringing ill-luck.
           It can't be sold
for the marriage was good in its own
time, though that time is gone.
           Could some artificer
beat into it bright stones, transform it

into a dazzling circlet no one could take
for solemn betrothal or to make promises
living will not let them keep? Change it
into a simple gift I could give in friendship?

A Son

A flamey monster–plumage and blossoms
        fountaining forth
                        from her round head,
        her feet
                squeezing mud between their toes,
        a tail of sorts
                        wagging hopefully
        and a heart of cinders and dreamstuff,
                flecked with forever molten gold,
            drumrolling in her breast–
bore a son.

            His father? A man
not at ease with himself,
half-monster too,
half earnest earth,
                    fearful of monsterhood;
                    kindly, perplexed, a fire
                    smouldering.

The son
        took, from both monsters, feathers
        of pure flame,

        and from his mother,
                        alchemical gold,
        and from his father,
                        the salt of earth:

        a triple goodness.

If to be artist
is to be monster,
he too was monster. But from his self
uprose a new fountain,
       of wisdom, of in-seeing, of wingéd justice
       flying unswerving
       into the heart.

               He and compassion
were not master and servant,
       servant and master,
but comrades in pilgrimage.

What My House Would Be Like If It Were A Person

This person would be an animal.
This animal would be large, at least as large
as a workhorse. It would chew cud, like cows,
having several stomachs.
No one could follow it
into the dense brush to witness
its mating habits. Hidden by fur,
its sex would be hard to determine.
Definitely it would discourage
investigation. But it would be, if not teased,
a kind, amiable animal,
confiding as a chickadee. Its intelligence
would be of a high order,
neither human nor animal, elvish.
And it would purr, though of course,
it being a house, you would sit in *its* lap,
not it in yours.

Artist to Intellectual (Poet to Explainer)

i

'The lovely *obvious!* The feet
supporting the body's tree and its crown
of leafy flames, of fiery
knowledge roaming
into the eyes,
that are lakes, wells, open
skies! The lovely
evident, revealing
everything, more mysterious
than any
clueless inscription scraped in stone.
The ever-present, constantly vanishing,
carnal enigma!'

ii

'Do I prophesy? It is
for now, for no future.
Do I envision? I envision
what every seed
knows, what shadow
speaks unheard
and will not repeat.
My energy
has not direction,
tames no chaos,
creates, consumes, creates
unceasing its own
wildfires that none
shall measure.'

iii

'Don't want to measure, want to be
the worm slithering wholebodied
over the mud and grit of what
may be a mile,
may be forever–pausing
under the weeds to taste
eternity, burrowing
down not along,
rolling myself
up at a touch, outstretching
to undulate in abandon to exquisite rain,
returning, if so I desire, without
reaching that goal the measurers
think we must head for. Where is
my head? Am I not
worm all over? My own
orient!'

The Poet Li Po Admiring a Waterfall

*Improvisation on a Xmas card for the
composer David del Tredici, at Yaddo,
Xmas, 1975*

And listening to its
Japanese blues, the bass
of its steady plunging
tones of dark,
and within their roaring:
strands of thin
foamwhite, airbright
light inwoven!–all
falling

so far
so deep,
his two
acorn-hatted infant
acolytes fear
he will long to
fly like spray
and fall too, off
the sloping, pale
edge of the world,
entranced!

Postcard

The sunshine is wild here!
It laps our feet!
Wavelets of sunshine!
Spiky wavelets!
The sunshine snaps at our toes!
Thick handfuls of sunshine freeze
our fingers like ice,
like burning ice cream!
Farewell!
The towers of the city across
the gulf of sunshine are wavering!

Hidden Monsters at the Mount Auburn Cemetery.
A Found Poem.

I looked after the carving while it was executing at
                                        the prison,
and found it necessary to make only one slight deviation
                                        from the model.
You may recollect that in most of the Egyptian cornices
there is on each side of the globe, a fabulous sort
                                        of animal,
with an inflated body, and a head like a serpent or
                                        crocodile . . .
As it was suggested that an uncouth Egyptian idol
might give offense to some persons,
I sought for some way of modifying it,
which might cover this difficulty
without departing from the main design.
I accordingly instructed the workmen to introduce
an Egyptian Lotus on each side,
the flower of which falls so as to conceal
the head of the monster,

leaving the spectator to imagine what he pleases behind it.

Dr. Jacob Bigelow to H.A.S. Dearborn,
Boston, January 13th, 1833

Blake's Baptismal Font°

Behind the Tree the hands
of Eve and Adam almost
                        meet.
Only a single thick

° See note on page 276.

rope of serpent
divides them.

Adam holds
his other hand on his heart
                    in fear
as Eve stretches out *her* other hand
across the front of the Tree
        to offer him knowledge.
The apple the serpent holds in its mouth
and the twin apples of her breasts are all
exact replicas of the apple she holds.

Four prehensile, elegant, practical feet
stand among roots.
Above the heads
                of man and woman and serpent,
dense leaves and a crown of apples hide
the font and its bas-relief stories–
            the sky's dome
upturned, an unknown cosmos.

For X . . .

I've never written poems for you, have I.
You rarely read poems,
your mind thrives
on other fruits and grains:

but just this once
a poem; to say:

As unthought gestures, turns of
common phrase, reveal
the living of life–
pathos, courage, comedy;

as in your work you witness
and show others
people's ordinary and always strange
histories;

so you give me from myself
an open secret,

a language other than my language, poetry,
in which to rest myself with you,

in which to laugh with you;

a cheerful privacy
like talking Flemish on a bus in Devon.

Love Poem

'We are good for each other.'
X

What you give me is

the extraordinary sun
splashing its light
                    into astonished trees.

A branch
of berries, swaying

under the feet of a bird.

I know
other joys–they taste
bitter, distilled as they are
from roots, yet I thirst for them.

But you–
you give me
the flash of golden daylight
in the body's
midnight,
warmth of the fall noonday
between the sheets in the dark.

Chant: Sunset, Somerville, Late Fall '75

Cloudy luminous rose-mallow sundown,
                     suffusing the whole
roof-and-branch-interrupted lofty
air, blue fishscale slates,
wires, poles, trolleycars, flash
of window,
rectangular Catholic tall campanile abstracted
above North Cambridge, people heads down
leaving the store with groceries, bathed–
all!–utterly
           in this deepening, poised,
           fading-to-ivory oxbowed river of
light,
one drop
of crimson lake to a brimming
floodwater chalice
and we at the lees of it–ah,
no need to float, to long
to float upward, into it, sky itself
is floating us into the dusk, we are motes
of gold brushed from the fur
of mothwings, night is
breathing
close to us,
dark, soft.

LIFE IN THE FOREST

For Jon:
·
Brother in dream
·
Sometime lover
·
Friend
·
Imaginer
·

Movement

Towards not being
anyone else's center
of gravity.
        A wanting
to love: not
to lean over towards
an other, and fall,
but feel within one
a flexible steel
upright, parallel
to the spine but
longer, from which to stretch;
one's own
grave springboard; the outflying spirit's
vertical trampoline.

Spirit has been alone
of late. Built a house
of fallen leaves
among exposed tree-roots.
Plans dreamily
to fetch water

from a stone well.
Sleeps
hungrily.
        Waking,
is mute,
listening. Spirit
doesn't know
what the sound will be,
song or cry.
Perhaps

one word. Holds
at heart a
red thread, winding

back to the world,

to one who holds
the far end,
far off.
            Spirit
throws off the quilts
when darkness
is very heavy,

shuffles among
the leaves
upstairs and down
waiting.

Wants
the thread to vibrate

again. Again! Crimson!

Meanwhile refuses
visitors, asks
those who come
no questions,
answers none. Digs in
for winter,
             slowly.

Life in the Forest

The woman whose hut was mumbled by termites
–it would have to go,
  be gone,
  not soon, but some day:
  she knew it and shrugged–
had friends among the feathers,
quick hearts.

And among crickets too,
brown and faithful,
creviced at hearthside winters.

But her desire
fixed on a chrysalis.

              How Eternity's
silver blade filed itself fine
on the whetstone of her life!
              How the deep velours
of the wings, the mystery of the feelers,
              drew amazed cries from her

164

when the butterfly came forth
and looked at her, looked at her, brilliantly gazing.
                    It was a man, her own size,
and touched her everywhere.

And how, when Time, later,
once the Eternal had left to go wandering,
knocked and knocked on her door, she smiled,
                    and would not open!

The trees
began to come in of themselves, evenings.
The termites labored.
The hut's green moss of shadows
gave harbor
to those who sheltered her.

She was marked
by the smile within her. Its teeth
bit and bit at her sense of loss.

                                        Letter

You in your house among your roommate's plants
that seem at times, you tell me, an overgrown thicket
                    of assertive leaves,

obtrusive–

are lonely. Deeply,
with a plumb-line
stillness.
        I feel it,
two miles away.

You work, your typewriter clatters cheerfully,
scenes evolve; while Dylan sings on,

                     and the record-changer
proceeds with its duties.
But underneath all is that stillness.
You hear your own heartbeats.

                   And I in my house
of smaller plants, many books, colored rugs,
my typewriter silent,
                have been searching out for you,
though I forget how we came to speak of it, the name
of the three beings who shared
just the one fateful eye between them,
spitefully taking turns. I found them:
they were the Graiae, the Grey ones, who guarded
their sisters the Gorgons. Perseus outwitted them,
the hero who rescued Andromeda; he stole
that sinister vigilant marble, using the craftiness
that is given to heroes in time of need.

Also I found (looking for something else)
in the long, grown-up, valedictory poem
close to the end of *A Child's Garden of Verses*–
yes, in that elegy,
not in the black shadows of a drawing memory collaged
from the illustrations to earlier pages–
                      I found
Babylon, and candles,
             and the long night.

I too today,
the wind and the rain transforming
my house to an island, a bare rock in the sea,
am alone
and know I'm alone,
                silent within the gusting weather.
The plumb-line
doesn't swing, it
comes to rest

a cold small weight
hung from its faithful cord
level with heart's core.

A Wanderer

i

The iris hazel, pupils
large in their round blackness,
his eyes
do see me,
he hugs me
tightly, but

he turns away,
he takes his grief
home with him,
my half of it
hides behind me as I
wave, he waves,
and it and I
close my door for the night.

ii

He has taken his sorrow
away to strangers.
They form a circle around it,
listening, touching,
drawing it forth.

It weeps among them,
begins to shed
cloaks and shawls, its old
gray and threadbare twisted bandages,

and show
pale skin, dark wounds.

My arms are empty,
my warm bed's empty,
I say no
to the lovers who want to warm themselves
in me.
       I want

to lie alone, dreaming awhile
about that ring dance,
that round
I don't know how to sing,
that language
strangers talk to him in,
speaking runes to his sorrow.

A Pilgrim Dreaming

By the fire light
of Imagination, brand
held high in the pilgrim's
upraised hand, he sees,
not knowing what boundaries it may have,

a well, a pool or river—
water's darkly shining
mirror, offering
his sought-for Self.

O, he silently
cries out, reaching gladly.
But *O,* again: he sees
dimly, beside the knowledge
he has sought, another:

now he hesitates–
she whose face attentively
looks from the water up to him,
tutelary spirit of this place,
of the water-mirror,

who is she. It is
not a question.
It is a question
and troubles him. The flames

flutter and fail, Imagination
falters. His image
vanishes, he is left
in a vague darkness.

Then it is
he fears the glimmering presence,
her image
vanished like his own,
yet not utterly. Only

when with his breath
he reawakens fire, the light
of vision, will he once more

know the steady look, the face
of his own life. Only in presence
of his Self
can he look gladly
at that other face,

the mirror's gazing spirit,
mute, eloquent, weak, a power,
powerless,
yet giving
what he desires, if he gives light.

Part I–December

A child, no-one to stare, I'd run full tilt to a tree,
hug it, hold fast, loving the stolid way it
stood there, girth
arms couldn't round,
                    the way
only the wind made it speak, gave it
an autumn ocean of thoughts
creaking on big wings into the clouds, or rolling
in steady uncountable sevens in
to the wild cliffs when I shut my eyes.

. . . .

If I came to a brook, off came my shoes,
looking could not be enough–
or my hands at least must be boats or fish for a minute,
to know the purling water at palm and wrist.
My mind would sink like a stone
and shine underwater,
dry dull brown
                    turned to an amber glow.

. . . .

My friend . . . My friend, I would like
to talk to myself about you: beginning
with your bright, hazel, attentive eyes,
the curving lines of your mouth.
I would like to ponder the way
I have grown so slowly aware those lines
are beautiful, generous. Energy lights your
whole face, matching
the way you walk. A gradual seeing,
not in a phantom flash of storm . . .

But I'm not ready
to speak about you,
Not yet.
Perhaps I will never be ready,
nor you to be spoken of.

. . . .

Whether or not I find
words for you, to tell myself who you are,

I shan't mistake you
for a tree to cling to. Let me speak of you
as of a river:
quick-gleaming, conjuring
little pyramids of light that pass
in laughter from braided ripple to ripple;
but pausing, dark
in pools where boughs
lean over;
but never
at a standstill—

. . . .

        I don't know how deep,
how cold. I want
to touch it, drink of it, open mouth
bent to it.

Sometimes as a child
I'd slip on the rocks and fall in.
Never mind.
I wanted to know
the river's riveriness with my self,

be stone or leaf, sink or be
swept downstream
to spin and vanish, spin

and hover, spin
and sweep on beyond sight.

Part II–February

'And what if the stream
is shallow?'

Then I will wade in it.

'–the current only a ripple
that will not bear you?'

I'll make my way,
not leaf nor stone, a human,
step by step, walking,
slipping, scrambling,
seeking the depth

where the waters will summon themselves
to lift me
off my feet.

I am looking always
for the sea.

. . . .

Let me say
it is I who am a river.
Someone
is walking along
the shore of me.

He is looking
sometimes at my surface,
the lights and the passing
wingshadows,

172

sometimes
through me, and down
towards rocks and sand,

sometimes across me
into another country.

Does he see me?

. . . .

I met a friend
as I walked by the river that runs
through my mind.

Or he himself
was the river,

for this river
rises in metamorphosis
when some confluence
of wills occurs far-off,
          where the gods are,

and could appear
as a man,
as my friend–

who would be unaware
then, of his river-nature,

his own eyes (not
hazel, as I thought,
but topaz, are they?)
fixed rather upon flames,

for it may be
fire, not a river flowing,
flickers and glows in his mind,

173

while to me, drawn
to water by the pull
of searching roots,

he would seem
a river, or a man
gazing searchingly
into the river,
a fellow-wanderer . . .

Part III–April

But what are
            the trees to which–
            (to whom, were they not beings,
            impassive but sentient? 'Dreamy, gloomy,
            friendly . . .')
                        –I ran long ago, and still
when I'm alone, embrace sometimes, shyly,
not impulsively: pensively;
      what within me or in those I love, or who draw me
towards themselves (as water
is pulled by roots out of the soil, to rise up
up, and up
            into the tower of the tree)
–what is the counterpart, then,
in these or myself,
to imagined, retrieved, pines and oaks of the past
uttering ocean on inland gusts of autumnal wind?
(Eyes closed, eyes closed,
                        swaying as they swayed,
            listening with the heart to envisioned breakers,
the senses confounded, my breathing
breathing with boughs' tossing
until delight
broke in me into a dance,
unwitnessed, secret, whirling,
as if I became

174

a heap of firstfallen leaves
                              to eddy and fly
joyfully over the field
and scatter–)
What within us is tree?
                              What
cannot be budged, the stock
'not moved' that stands and yet
draws us
        into ourselves, centers us,
        never rebuffs us, utters
our wildest dreams for us, dreams
of oceanic blessing,
our hymns of pure being?

. . . .

Neither mighty tree,
                        sounding
                                    of ocean
nor river flooding toward
                              sea-depths;

my self is a grey-barked sapling
of a race that needs
                        a hundred years' growth
close to water.
                    Its dryad soul
dreams of plunging, of
swallow-diving off the pliant
twigs of its crown
into fathomless caverns, sliding
through yielding glass.
Its roots
        inch their toes
toward hidden streamlets
planning to pull them
                              drop by drop
up through clay, gravel, thick

topsoil, to slake
                sip by sip
tree-thirst, flesh of wood that harbors
that dreamer.

. . . .

Are you flame among the branches,
unaware? You move flickering, swift, restless
in your own life,
but I see no path behind you
of blackened leaves.
                Yourself, is it,
you burn?

. . . .

Friend,
        more than friend,
                        less than friend,
in dream I came to the home of your family
to deliver a message.
Messenger of the gods, I knew
nothing of what I was to tell. Only those
who received it would comprehend
what it was.
                You had a sister,
who resembled you–
                tall, curly-haired, with an aquiline, questing nose,
a sharp-edged presence, restless, charged
with some half-concealed wistful desire–
but resembled me too,
as if she and I were sisters: I knew this
though I know little of my own
presence, what it is.
                        She was kind to me,
welcomed me warmly into the house
which was stirring with eager people, cousins,
                                        grandparents,

aunts and uncles, all talking quickly,
                              moving through the rooms.
Everywhere green plants hung from baskets,
swaying in fish-swift ripples of light
as the family passed to and fro
smiling, vehement, pursuing
shining ribbons of concept that crisscrossed in mid-air
like strong fibers of gossamer.
I could not see you
though you were surely there
somewhere in that place where it was clear you belonged;
but your sister drew me kindly into the midst
and brought me the cup that is brought
to messengers from distant places, before they must
                                                    speak.

. . . .

I see for sure now
          beginning to speak of you, ready,
          for a moment's grace, to speak at last
          of what I don't know but see in the dark:
the flame is Imagination's flame
that burns your spirit.
                              When you
are present, but
not present,
                              when you
scarcely sink into sleep
but merely rest in the deadman's float
among waves that never for a moment
let up their jostling,
                    where you are
                    is with the envisioning fire
inside the cave of the mind
where Images ride to the hunt on the creviced walls
as the flame struggles out of the smoke.
All about you is watery, within you lies the dark
cave, and the fire.

177

. . . .

When you love me well
        it is when
        Imagination has flicked
                            its fire-tongue over you,
                            you are freed
        by that act of the mind
                            to act.
You have
those moments of absolute sureness,
exploding, golden, in the shifting, smoky, uncertain
                            dimensions of the cave,
when the hunter's
                quarry is under his hand,
                breathing, trembling, its heart
racing, and he puts his mark on it,
letting it go until it returns of its own
accord;
        those instants
when the Creative Spirit, sisterly,
takes a Wanderer's cold and burning hand
in hers
and they enter the dance.

Magic

The brass or bronze cup, stroked at the rim,
round and around, begins
to hum,
   the hum slowly
buzzes more loudly, and rapidly now
becomes
    the clang of the bell of the
    deep world, unshaken, sounding
    crescendo out of its wide mouth
         one note,
   continuous,
      gong
   of the universe, neither beginning nor ending,
but heard
only those times we take
the cup and stroke
the rim,
diminuendo,
only seeming
to cease when we cease
to listen . . .

CANDLES IN BABYLON (1982)

.

Through the midnight streets of Babylon
between the steel towers of their arsenals,
between the torture castles with no windows,
we race by barefoot, holding tight
our candles, trying to shield
the shivering flames, crying
'Sleepers Awake!'
                    hoping
the rhyme's promise was true,
that we may return
from this place of terror
home to a calm dawn and
the work we had just begun.

WANDERER'S DAYSONG

Dwellers at the Hermitage

Grief sinks and sinks
into the old mineshaft
under their house,
how deep, who knows.
When they have need
for it, it's there.

Their joys
refused to share themselves,
fed from the hand
of one alone, browsed
for days in dappled
pathless woods
untamed.

Sorrow
is what one shares,
they say;
and happiness, the wistful gold
of our solitudes, is what
our dearest lovers,
our wingéd friends,
leave with us, in trust.

The Soothsayer

My daughters, the old woman says, the weaver
        of fictions, tapestries
        from which she pulls
        only a single thread each day, pursuing
        the theme at night–
my daughters? Delicate bloom
of polished stone. Their hair
ripples and shines like water, and mine
is dry and crisp as moss in fall.

Trunk, limbs, bark; roots under all of it:
the tree I am, she says, blossoms year after year,
random, euphoric;
the bees are young, who nuzzle their fur
into my many fragile hearts.
My daughters
have yet to bear
their fruit,
they have not imagined
the weight of it.

The Chill

Mother and Father have fulfilled their promise:
        the overture, the rise of the curtain, the imagined pomp
        of magic and artifice, all
        glows, as if music
        were made of candle flames, all
        flows, as if dancers
        were golden oil of music,
        the theater's marvelous smell is also
        the prickle of crimson velvet on bare skin–but
            at the marrow of all this joy, the child

185

is swept by a sudden
chill of patience: notices wearily
the abyss that Time
opens before it.
                         Careful, careful–
no one must share
this knowledge.
The child tenderly, tense with protective love,
guards their innocent happiness,
            kind Father,
            kind Mother.
                         Quickly! Back to the long-desired,
the even-better-than-hoped-for treat.
                         Has one not run
                         more than once
            back from a strip of woods to open sunlight,
            hastily laughing, uttering
            not a word about
                               white
                                         bones
            strewn in ivy,
                         and old feathers, raggéd?

Poet and Person

I send my messages ahead of me.
You read them, they speak to you
in siren tongues, ears of flame
spring from your heads to take them.

When I arrive, you love me,
for I sing those messages you've
leaned by heart, and bring,
as housegifts, new ones. You hear

186

yourselves in them,
self after self. Your solitudes
utter their runes, your own
voices begin to rise in your throats.

But soon you love me less.
I brought with me
too much, too many laden coffers,
the panoply of residence,

improper to a visit.
Silks and furs, my enormous wings,
my crutches, and my spare crutches,
my desire to please, and worse–

my desire to judge what is right.

I take up
so much space.
You are living on what you can find,
you don't want charity, and you can't
support lingering guests.

When I leave, I leave
alone, as I came.

The Passing Bell

One by one
they fall away–

all whom they really
wanted to keep. People.
Things that were more than things.

187

The dog, the cat,
the doll with a silk dress,
the red penknife:
those were the first to go.

Then father, mother,
sister, brother,
wife and husband.
Now the child.

The child is grown,
the child is gone,
the child has said,
Don't touch me, don't call me,

your lights have gone out,
I don't love you.
No more.

The distant child
casts a tall shadow:
that's the dark.
And they are small.

The world is brittle,
seamed with cracks,
ready to shatter. Now

the old man steps
into a boat,
rows down the rainy street.
Old woman, she climbs up

into the steeple's eye.
Transmogrified, she's
the clapper of the bell.

The tolling begins.

Try to remember, every April, not this one only
you feel you are walking underwater
in a lake stained by your blood.

When the east wind rips the sunlight
your neck feels thin and weak, your clothes
don't warm you.

You feel you are lurching away from
deft shears, rough hands, your fleece
lies at the shepherd's feet.

And in the first warm days each step
pushes you against a weight,
and you don't want

to resist that weight,
you want to stop, to return
to darkness
          –but treaties made
over your head force you to
waver forward.

Yes, this year you feel
at a loss, there is no Demeter
to whom to return

if for a moment you saw
yourself as Persephone.
It is she, Demeter, has gone
          down to the dark.

Or if it is Orpheus drawing you forth,
Eurydice,
he is inexorable, and does not look back
to let you go.

You are appalled to consider you may be destined
to live to a hundred.
But it is April,

there is nothing unique in your losses,
your pain is commonplace
and your road ordained:

your steps will hurt you,
you will arrive
as usual

at some condition you name *summer:*

an ample landscape,
voluptuous, calm,
of large, very still trees,
water meadows, dreamy
savannah distances,

where you will gather strength,
pulling ripe fruit from the boughs,
for winter and spring,
forgotten seasons.

Try to remember it is always this way.
You live
this April's pain
now,

you will come
to other Aprils,
each will astonish you.

People like me can't feel
the full rush of air around us as we
plunge into swansdown billows of
dustgold fathomless happenstance–

                   we leap but
we've known the leaden no-light
that's not darkness, that is
eclipse. When green
loses its green spirit. When vertigo
takes the wheeling swifts and drops them like separate
pebbles of rain. When rain
begins and stops, appalled at the discourse of bones it makes
on cracked clay. That no-light blunted us.

Yes, and we've known, we know
every day, our tall mothers and fathers
are gone, no one
has known us always,
we are ancient orphans,
parchment skins stretched upon crutches,
inscribed with epitaphs.

When mirrors tell us white beards
have not yet appeared from within us

nor pendulous breasts
hung themselves on our torsos like bundles
of parched herbs,

when the sun
gnaws its way out of its cage again,

when the skylark
tears itself out of our throats,

191

we do leap, we do
plunge into skylake's
haze of promise. But we feel

along with the air rushing, our own breath
rushing
out of us.
            See
for an instant the arc of
our vanishing.

The Dragonfly-Mother*

I was setting out from my house
to keep my promise

but the Dragonfly-Mother stopped me.

I was to speak to a multitude
for a good cause, but at home

the Dragonfly-Mother was listening
not to a speech but to the creak of
                stretching tissue,
tense hum of leaves unfurling.

Who is the Dragonfly-Mother?
What does she do?

She is the one who hovers
on stairways of air,
                sometimes almost
grazing your cheekbone,
she is the one who darts unforeseeably

* See note on page 276.

into unsuspected dimensions,

who sees in water
her own blue fire zigzag, and lifts
her self in laughter
into the tearful pale sky

that sails blurred clouds in the stream.

.

She sat at my round table,
we told one another dreams,
I stayed home breaking my promise.

When she left I slept
three hours, and arose

and wrote. I remember the cold
Waterwoman, in dragonfly dresses

and blue shoes, long ago.
She is the same,

whose children were thin,
left at home when she went out dancing.
She is the Dragonfly-Mother,

that cold
is only the rush of air

swiftness brings.
There is a summer
over the water, over

the river mirrors
where she hovers, a summer
fertile, abundant, where dreams
grow into acts and journeys.

193

Her children
are swimmers, nymphs and newts, metamorphic.
                              When she tells
her stories she listens; when she listens
she tells you the story you utter.

                        •

When I broke my promise,
and slept, and later
cooked and ate the food she had bought
and left in my kitchen,

I kept a tryst with myself,
a long promise that can be fulfilled
only poem by poem,
broken over and over.

                        I too,
a creature, grow among reeds,
            in mud, in air,
in sunbright cold, in fever
of blue-gold zenith, winds
of passage.

            Dragonfly-Mother's
a messenger,
if I don't trust her
I can't keep faith.

                    There is a summer
in the sleep
of broken promises, fertile dreams,
acts of passage, hovering
journeys over the fathomless waters.

There are times
        no one seems to notice
                        when I move weightlessly
not flying exactly
                but stepping as if in
                                7 league boots–
yet not
        leagues at a time,
                        merely a modest matter of
feet or at most yards.
I don't
        know how it is that
                        no one sees it, or
could it be they do, and don't
                mention it
                        from embarrassment?
Certainly
        it is strange, I know,
                        and yet
there's no need for anyone to
                feel afraid. I prefer
not to suppose
                envy could cause their silence.
                                        No,
more likely it's only
                so improbable,
                        they don't believe
their eyes.
For myself, I confess,
                        it is a
                        great delight–
the springiness,
                the soft
                        swing of it.
Especially I like
                to traverse

a landscape this way
when there is no one
looking.
There is
a low hill rising from marshland I've been to lately
at twilight, an hour
of mist and mauve loomings of
vast and benevolent
ancient trees—
I returned
only when sensing myself
too close to the deepening water.

On the Way

On the way to the
valley of transformation
one arrives sometimes at
those evenings, late, the mirror gives one,
(softlit, and folds or falls
of silk or wool
conspiring like the eyes of
loyal friends)
when one's own image greets one with pleasure.
Pleasure! How one smiles back, still hearing
goodnights and laughter,
how one turns up the radio's midnight blues
and dances,
and checks the mirror and sees,
yes, one is dancing there, looking
just the way dancers do when one watches
wistfully from the outskirts of music.
On the way down there are
these way stations
where goodbyes
are festive lanterns by the edge of a lake

and the face in the glass has shed its agelines as if
they were the mirage.

The Art of the Octopus: Variations on a Found Theme

The octopus is a solitary creature, and for it,
*   any shelter it can find is home.*
Connoisseur of continents,
it embraces gratefully the flatlands where shadows
dance the largesse of sky and transpose
the gestures of clouds whose wagon trains
roll across domed springtime,

while simultaneously
another caressive tentacle
strokes the steel girders of the mountains'
refusal to budge, admiring their steadfast ranks,
their doctrine of patience.

When it gave up its protective shell it developed
many skills and virtues.

It can, for example, curl itself small
to live in attics where daybreak
is an alertness of red rooftiles that a moment ago
were a vague brown at the western window,
or it can untwine, stretching out starbeams into voluptuous
unexplored chains of high-vaulted thronerooms
beyond the scan of hurried, bone-aching throngs
below in the long streets.
                              These are skills.
Virtues? Transparently
it ingests contrast, regarding it humbly
as joy. Nourished,
it gives forth peculiar light, a smoky radiance.
Some see this aura. Some think it poisonous,

others desire it. Of those who enter
that bright cloud, some vanish. Others begin
to grow long, wavering, extra arms, godlike,
so that at last they touch
many things at once, and reach
towards everything; they too begin
the solitary dance.

The May Mornings

May mornings wear
light cashmere shawls of quietness,
brush back waterfalls of
burnished silk from
clear and round brows.
When we see them approaching
over lawns, trailing
dewdark shadows and footprints,
we remember, ah,
yes, the May mornings,
how could we have forgotten,
what solace it would have been
to think of them,
what solace
it would be in the bitter violence
of fire then ice again we
apprehend–but
it seems the May mornings
are a presence known
only as they pass
lightstepped, seriously smiling, bearing
each a leaflined basket
of wakening flowers.

Rain Spirit Passing

Have you ever heard the rain at night
streaming its flaxen hair against
the walls of your house?

Have you ever heard the rain at night
drifting its black, shiny, seaweed hair
through multistoreyed arcades of leaves?

And have you risen then
from bed and felt your way
to the window, and raised the blind, and seen

       stillness, unmisted moonlight, the air
       dry? Street and garden
       empty and silent?

You had been lying awake; the rain
was no dream. Yet where is it?

When did that rain descend and descend,
filling your chalices
until their petals loosened

and wafted
down to rest
on grass and the wet ground,

and your roots in their burrows
stretched and sighed?

II

PIG DREAMS

Her Destiny

The beginning: piglet among piglets,
the soft mud caking
our mother's teats.
Sweetsqueal, grunt:
her stiff white lashes, the sleepy
glint of her precious
tiny eyes.

·

But I am Sylvia. Chosen.
I was established
pet. To be
the pig of dreams, the pig
any of us could be,
  taken out of the sty,
  away from the ravaged soil of pig-yards,
  freed from boredom and ugliness.
I was chosen to live without dread of slaughter.

·

For three days, after they took me,
I hungered. Nowhere a teat to suck from,
no piglet siblings to jostle and nudge.
At last
  in the full moon's sacred light
  in the human room where I'd run
  in circles till my tapping trotters
  almost gave way,
the He-human

                    naked and white as my
                    lost mother,
bent on all-fours over my untouched bowl,
his beard a veil before me,
and with musical loud sounds of guzzling
showed me *eating*. Gave me
the joy of survival.

                              •

Quicklearner, soon
I could hold my shit.
I was rocked in warm
human arms.
I liked laps, the thighs
of humans.
Cuddling.
          Every pig
could be cuddled if there were justice.
          Every human
could have its intelligent pig,
          every pig
its dextrous human. Our lives
would be rich as creamy corn,
tasty as acorns.

Dogbrothers

Pigalone. Sylvia.
Sylvia Orphan Onlypig.
Even my She-human's lap
could not console.
But then I found
my Dogbrothers.
Bark and growl,
dog-laugh, waving

tails and the joy
of chasing, of whirling,
squealing, my dainty trotters
trilling beneath me
sharp and sure!
Of huddling to doze
in warm quickbreathing
muddle of dogs,
almost believing
I, Sylvia,
am dog not pig.

The Catpig

John the Cat
is most my brother,
almost pig

even though he
leaps among branches,
climbs to high shelves,
is silky.

Black and white Catpig,
I outgrew you,
but once we matched.

She-human gave us
our milk from
our pitcher.

Quiet we sat
under the sumacs of Vermont
and watched

the birds leave,
the first snow
pepper each other's
somber faces.

Winterpig

At the quick of winter
moonbrightest
snowdeepest

we would set out.
I'd run up my ramp
into the pickup,

we'd rattle and shake
two midnight miles
to the right hill.

Then on foot,
slither and struggle
up it—

they'd
ready their sled
and toboggan down

and I'd
put down my nose and
spread my ears and

tear down beside them,
fountains of snow
spurting around me:

I and my Humans
shouting, grunting,
the three of us

wild with joy,
just missing
the huge maples.

Yes, over and over
up to the top of the
diamond hill–

the leanest, the fastest,
most snow-and-moon-and-midnight-bewitched
pig in the world!

The Bride

They sent me away to be bred.
I was afraid, going down the ramp
from the truck to the strange barn,
I tried to run for the farmyard–strangers
shouted, they drove me inside.

In the barn a beautiful, imperious boar
dwelt in majesty. They brought me to him.
In the hot smell of him, I who was delicate,
        Sylvia the pet,
                    who smelled of
            acorns and the windscoured pasture,
        I, Sylvia the Dreamer,
was brought low,
was brought
into the depths
of desire.

I steeped my soul
                in the sweet dirt,
                        the stench of
        My Lord Boar

                        •

Terrible, after the sensuous dark,
                the week of passion and feasting,
–terrible my return.
I screamed when they dragged me
outdoors to the truck. Harsh light
jumped at my eyes. My body's weight
sagged on my slender legs.

In the house of My Lord Boar
I had eaten rich swill.

Back home, I headed for my
private house, the house of Sylvia–
and my swill-swollen body
                would not enter,
                could not fit.

In shame I lay
many nights
on the ground outside my Humans' window
and passed my days silent and humble
in the bare pasture, until I was lean again,
                until I could enter
                my maiden chamber once more.

But now I carried in me
the fruit of my mating.

My piglets cling to me,
perfect, quickbreathing, plump–
kernels of pearly sweetcorn,
milky with my milk.

These shall I housetrain, I swear it,
these shall dwell like their mother
among dextrous humans, to teach them
pig-wisdom. O Isis, bless
thy pig's piglets.

Her Secret

In the humans' house
fine things abound:
furniture, rugs by the hearth,
bowls and pitchers, freezer and fridge,
closets of food, baskets of apples,
the Musical Saw on which
my He-human plays
                    the songs I dream . . .

In my neat A-frame
they think there is nothing,
only the clean straw of my bed.
But under the floor I gather
beautiful tins, nutshells, ribbons,
shining buttons, the thousand baubles
a pig desires.

They are well hidden.
Piglets shall find one day
an inheritance of shapes,
textures, mysterious substances–

Rubber! Velvet! Aluminum! Paper!

Yes, I am founding,
    stick by stick,
    wrapper by wrapper,
    trinkets, toys–
Civilization!

Her Nightmare

The dream is blood: I swim,
which is forbidden to pigs,
and the doom comes: my sharp
flailing feet cut
into my thick throat
and the river water
is stained, and fills, and
thickens with bright blood
and darkens, and I'm
choking, drained,
too weak to heave
out of the sticky
crimson mud, and
I sink and sink in it
screaming, and then
voiceless, and
when I wake it's
the dark of the moon.

Yet, when I was young,
not knowing the prohibition,
I did swim. The corn
was tall, and my skin
was dry as old
parchment of husks,
the creviced earth
scorched, and no rain

had fallen
for long and long:
when my She-human plunged
into the lovely
cool and wet river,
I too
plunged, and swam.
It was easy to me
as if the water
were air, and I
a young bird in flight.
My pig-wings
flailed, but my throat
was not slit, and we crossed
the river, and rested
under splashed leaves
on the far shore,
and I thought I would always
be Sylvia Waterpig.
O it was sweet
to be upborne
on the fresh-running current,
a challenge to push
across it and gain
the moss and shade.
I escaped
the doom
then.
　　　But I grew
heavier, thick in the throat,
properly pigshaped,
and learned the Law.
And now,
this dream, on some
black nights, fills up
my bowl of sleep
with terror,
with blood.

When they caressed
and held in loving arms
the small pig that I was,
I was so glad, I blessed
my singular fate.
How could I know
my Humans would not grow
to fit me, as I became
Sylvia the Sow?
He-and-She-Human stayed the same, and now
even look smaller.
Perhaps I should not have learned
to adore
pleasures that could not last?
I grew so fast.
My destiny
kept me lean, and yet
my weight increased.
Great Sylvia, I must stay
under the table at the humans' feast.
And once, scratching my back on it,
I made the table fall
dishes and all!
How could a cherished piglet
have grown so tall?

Her Sadness

When days are short,
mountains already
white-headed, the west
red in its branchy
leafless nest, I know

more than a simple
sow should know.

I know
the days of a pig—
and the days of dogbrothers, catpigs,
cud-chewing cowfriends—
are numbered,

even the days of
Sylvia the Pet,

even the days
of humans are numbered.
Already

laps are denied me,
I cannot be cuddled,
they scratch my ears
as if I were anypig, fattening for bacon.

I shall grow heavier still,
even though I walk
for miles with my Humans,
through field and forest.

Mortality
weighs on my shoulders,
I know
too much about Time for a pig.

Kaya, my gentle
        Jersey cowfriend,
                you are no pig,
you are slow to think,
            your moods
                are like rounded clouds
drifting over the pasture,
            casting
                pleasant shadows.
You lift your head
        slowly
            up from the grass
to greet me.
        Occupied
            with your cud, you are
all cow,
      yet we are friends,
              or even sisters.
We worship
        the same goddess,
            we look
to the same humans
        with love,
            for love.
When I tread
        the mud in pigpatterns
                after a shower,
my footprints shine
        and reflect the sky:
            in this
they resemble your huge
        kindly eyes.
            My own

are small,
          as befits a pig,
                    but I behold your steep
graygold side,
          a bulwark
                    beside me.

Her Delight

I, Sylvia, tell you, my piglets
it has been given me
to spend a whole day up to my snout
in the velvet wetness that is mud:

and to walk undriven, at dusk,
back to the human-house
and be welcomed there:

welcomed by humans and cats and dogs,
not reproached for my mantle
of graying mud:

welcomed, and given to eat
a food of human magic, resembling mud
and tasting
of bliss: and its holy name
is *chocolate*.

I, Sylvia, your mother,
have known
the grace of pig-joy.

Her Judgement

I love my own Humans and their friends,
but let it be said,
that my litters may heed it well,
their race is dangerous.

They mock the race of Swine, and call
'swinish' men they condemn.
Have they not appetites? Do *we*
plan for slaughter to fill our troughs?

Their fat ones, despised, waddle large-footed,
their thin ones hoard
inedible discs and scraps
called 'money.' Us they fatten,
us they exchange for this;

and they breed us not that our life
may be whole, pig-life
thriving alongside dog-life, bird-life,
grass-life, all
the lives of earth-creatures,

but that we may be devoured. Yet,
it's not being killed for food
destroys us. Other animals
hunt one another. But only Humans,

I think, first corrupt their prey
as we are corrupted, stuffed with temptation
until we can't move,

crowded until we turn on each other,
our name and nature abused.

It is their greed
overfattens us.
Dirt we lie in is

never unclean as their minds,
who take our deformed lives
without thought, without
respect for the Spirit Pig.

Pig-song

Walnut, hickory, beechmast,
apples and apples, a meadow
of applegrass dapple.
Walnut, hickory, beechmast.
And over the sunfall slope,
cool of the dark mudwallow.

Her Vision

My human love, my She-human,
speaks to me in Piggish. She knows
my thoughts, she sees my emotions
flower and fade, fade and flower
as my destiny unrolls
its carpet, its ice and apples.

Not even she
knows all my dreams.
Under the russet sky
at dusk
I have seen
the Great Boar pass

invisible save to me.

His tusks are
flecked with skyfoam.
His eyes
red stars.

Her Prayer

O Isis my goddess,
my goddess Isis,
forget not thy pig.

Isis Speaks

Sylvia, my faithful
Petpig, teacher
of humans, fount
of pig-wisdom:
you shall yet know
the grief of parting:
your humans, bowed with regret,
shall leave you.
But hear me,
this is no dream
the time shall come
when you shall dwell,
revered,
in a house of your own
even finer than that you have.
And though you no longer
enter the houses of humans,
in springtimes to come
your black hide shall be strewn
with constellations of blossom.
Yes, in the deep summers,
apples shall bounce on your roof,
the ripe and round
fruit of your own appletree.
There you shall live long, and at peace,
redreaming the lore of your destiny.

III

PEOPLE, PLACES, VISIONS

An Arrival (North Wales, 1897)

The orphan arrived in outlandish hat,
proud pain of new button boots.
Her moss-agate eyes
photographed views of the noonday sleepy town
no one had noticed. Nostrils flaring,
she sniffed odors of hay and stone,
                absence of Glamorgan coaldust,
and pasted her observations quickly
into the huge album of her mind.
Cousins, ready to back off like heifers
were staring:
              amazed, they received
the gold funeral sovereigns she dispensed
along with talk strange to them as a sailor's parrot.

Auntie confiscated the gold;
the mourning finery, agleam with jet,
was put by to be altered. It had been chosen
by the child herself and was thought
unsuitable. She was to be
the minister's niece, now,
not her father's daughter.
                  Alone,
she would cut her way through a new world's
graystone chapels, the steep and sideways
rockface cottages climbing
mountain streets,

enquiring, turning things over
in her heart,
            weeping only in rage or when

the choirs in their great and dark and
golden glory broke forth and the hills
skipped like lambs.

Visitant

i

From under wide wings of blackest velvet
—a hat such as the Duse might have worn—
peered out at me my mother,
tiny and silver-white, her ancient skin delicately
pink, her eyes their familiar very dark
pebble-green, flecked with amber. 'Mother,'
I cried or mumbled, urgent but even now
embarrassed, 'can you forgive me? Did you,
as I've feared and feared, feel betrayed
when I failed to be there
at the worst time, and returned
too late? Am I forgiven?' But she looked vague
under the velvet, the ostrich-down, her face small;
if she said mildly, 'There is nothing to forgive,'
it seemed likely she wasn't listening,
she was preoccupied with some concerns
of that other life, and when she faded
I was left unabsolved still, the raven drama
of her hat more vivid to me
than she in her polite inattention.
                              This, I told myself,
is fitting: if the dead live
for a while in partial semblances
of their past selves, they have no time
to bear grudges or to bless us;
their own present
holds them intent. Yet perhaps
sometimes they dream us.

ii

Another time she arrived
through the French window at home
(the house that has no place now
to *be* in, except in me)
with gypsy bundles, laughing, excited,
old but not ancient yet, strong,
a lone traveller.
                    It was clear
she had come only to visit,
not to remain–
'It was a long trip,' she said,
'from Heaven to here!'
and we hugged and laughed and were comfortable.
I saw each thread
in the tapestry seat of a forgotten chair,
cloudy figures in the marble mantelpiece,
each detail of that vanished room.
A joyful meeting, and she
incandescent with joy.
Yet next day my perplexed grief
did not lift away but still,
like a mallard with clipped wings
circles me summer and winter, settled
for life in my life's reedy lake.

Marta (Brazil, 1928)

A Saxon peasant girl
darning a sock, is telling
household tales to her sleepy daughters.
'So the roasting pan
said to the little brown hen–'
Looking up, she sees
their eyes have closed. No need

to tell what it said.
She trims the lamp,
sits in the small circle of gold;
dark of the room's corners
is in league with the dark outside.
The forest
is not the familiar forest of proper trees
whose names she knew,
woodland of midsummer Sunday walks,
Grandmother's märchen,
understandable dangers.
This is the jungle. Here
enormous dazzling butterflies lure her children
into the underbrush among the snakes.
Birds whose violent beauty
makes her long for the humble brown
of a thrush, scream through vines
that everywhere
hide those unknowable trees, trunks
masked in green and blossom, boughs
a ceiling of dense foliage and flashes
of hot sky. At times
a band of monkeys will leap
to the ridge of her roof, which Hans
has built like a homeland roof,
sound and well joined, from outlandish wood.
The creatures chatter:
their speech is strange, but no stranger
than what the people spoke whom they met
on the voyage and long journey to come here.
The clearing is still too small;
the jungle's too near, and grows
too fast, in endless rain and
steaming sunlight.
                    Oh,
where can he be? Three days already
have gone since he should have returned.
Oil for the lamp's
getting low . . . but what if right now

219

with a flashlight, he's making his way
back home? If there's no light,
it will seem like no welcome.

> And Hans never comes. Has drowned
> a mile from home, falling
> face forward into a rainswollen stream;
> feet entangled in ropes of vine,
> pack of supplies holding him down.
> Months will pass
> before his bones are discovered.

Marta rethreads her needle with bluegrey wool.
Her ears ache with listening:
silent slumber of Trudi,
just-audible breathing of Emmi,
unceasing hum and buzz and creaking and rustle
of Amazon forest,
                    thump of her heart.
Posture of waiting,
gesture of darning,
golden halo of lamplight–patient, unknowing,
Marta remains forever
a story without an ending,
broken off in the telling.

Winter Afternoons in the V. & A., pre-W.W.II°

Rain unslanting, unceasing,
darkening afternoon streets.

Within lofty and vast halls,
no one but I, except for

° See note on page 276.

the ancient guards, survivors
of long-ago battles, dozing

under a spell, perched
on the brittle chairs of their sinecure.

My shoes made no sound. I found
everything for myself,

everything in profusion.
Lace of wrought iron,

wrought jewels, Cellini's dreams,
disappearing fore-edge paintings,
chain mail, crinolines, Hokusai, Cotman.
Here was history

as I desired it: magical, specific,
jumbled, unstinting,

a world for the mind to sift
in its hourglass—now, while I was twelve,
or forever.

Heights, Depths, Silence, Unceasing Sound of the Surf

Are they birds or butterflies?
They are sailing, two, not a flock,
more silver-white than the high
clouds, blissful
solitary lovers in infinite azure.

Below them, within the reef,
green shallows, transparent.
                       Beyond,
bounded by angry lace that

flails the coral,
                    the vast,
ironic dark Pacific.

Tonga, 1979

Tropic Ritual

Full moon's sharp
command transforms
the leafspine of each
palmfrond to curved
steel: in absolute
allegiance, uncountable scimitars
hail the unwitnessed hour. The humans
have withdrawn,
curtained,
shuttered.
Stars fall, kamikaze
of ecstasy. The tide
submits and submits.
The moon exacts
penitent joy from lizards,
blood from dreaming women.
Dogs huddle
scared under the frangipani
which lets fall
silently one flower
into the sand.

Tonga, 1979

For Nikolai, Many Thousand Miles Away

The procession that has been crossing
the mountains of your mind since you were six
      and went to Mexico and Grandma showed you
      the trees or clouds moving
               along the horizon
traverses (clouds for now) this evening the Pacific,
up towards the Equator–horses, men,
centaurs, pilgrims, women with bundles, children;
refugees–or the wild heroes
of a mythology bearing its heavy altars
into the next of its worlds.
                In my hand,
a spiral shell I'd thought
an empty cornucopia
stirs–something looks out of it
and searches my palm with delicate
probing claws, annoyed.
Among the last stains of sundown
the stars return. I look about
for the Southern Cross, and am given–whist!
a shooting star.
          The great world and its wars
are a long way off, news wavers over
the radio and goes out, you and your life
are half a world distant, and in daylight.
                   Here
the surf the reef holds back
speaks without ceasing,
drawing breath
only to utter the next words of its rune.
Crickets begin–deaf to that great insistence–
to praise the night.
Above the dark ocean, over coral, over continents
the riders move, their power
felt but not understood, their will
remote.

For a Child

'In the field, a
        dark thing.'
'It was, oh, a
        bush or something.'

'No no, a
        dark thing,
something that could
        look at me.'

'Was it like a bear?
        Was it like a moose?'
'No, it was a dark thing
        keeping still to look at me.'

'Was it fierce? Was it foul?
        Was it going to leap upon you?'
'No, it was a shy thing,
        keeping still to look at me.'

Continent

for Dennis Lee

In Canada, a sense
of weight, of burden,
of under the belly of the live
animal land, a clod, or maybe
another beast that clutches
and hangs there. Florida
is its tail, muscular, succulent.

224

And in the U.S. sometimes
a draft, a current
of air, chills and heightens
the senses, an idea
of mind, of space, of less
dense flesh, something
not ethereal but poignant, a head
crowned with carved ice.

From the Train, Eastward

Furry blond wheatfield in
predawn light–I
thought it was a frozen pond

·

Small town, early morning.
No cars. Sunlit
children wait for the green light.

·

A deer! It leapt the fence,
scared of the train!
Did anyone else see it?

And twenty miles later
again a deer,
the exact same arc of gold!

·

After the trumpets, the
kettledrums, the
bold crescendo of mountains–

prairie subtleties, verbs
declined in gray,
green tones sustained, vast plainsong.

Old People Dozing

Their thoughts are night gulls
following the ferry, gliding
in and out of the window light
and through the reflected wall there, the door
that holds at its center
an arabesque of foam
always at vanishing point,
                              night gulls
that drift on airstream, reverse, swoop
out of sight, return, memory
moving again through the closed door,
white and effortless, hungry.

Eyes And No-Eyes

Sewing together the bits of data
abandoned by the retina.

Well, here was a hand.
We never did see
the lines of its palm.
But fate had inscribed the knuckles,
anyway. Remember?

Oh–that shine,
that reflection on the dark
T.V. screen.
What I was looking at

was a violet,
a shy symbol in purple. No,
a whole jarful of violets.

Their stems are long, they seek
light, perhaps maligned
by imputations of modesty:
nothing cares to be praised by mistake.

                    That shine
of noon on dark glass
distracted me. Plus what I knew.
How briefly
I focussed on pointed petals and
the white sanctum,
the gold herm within,
the magic eyelash-fine stripes of
darker purple
that led to it like strips of prayer rug.

Two Artists

i

                Rosalie Gascoigne.
Old nails, their large flat heads
a gray almost silver, bunched
in a blue-glazed stoneware pot–
flowers of the playful mind.
She has fenced one side
of an open invisible square with pickets of feathers–

and here's a bowlful of turret shells,
fingernail size, you can dip your hands in
as into millet, and hear
the music of jostled brittleness.
The room's a temple, the kind that's
thronged with casual, un-awestruck worshippers,
and crowded with small shrines, each
a surprise, and dedicated
each in its turn, to the principle
that nothing is boring, everything's
worth a second look. Presiding,
there's an escutcheon, its emblems
shapes unnamed by geometrists
slabs of old wood, weathered, residual,
formed by the absence of what was cut
for forgotten purpose, out of their past:
they meet now, austere, graceful,
transfigured by being placed,
being seen.

ii

Memphis Wood.

A studio looped with huge
hanks of wool, of scarlet,
jute and velvet and blue,
rough, braid, swathe, yardage–
textures and colors so profuse, who
can tell noun from adjective,
the process continuous, table, wall,
the woven stitched tied construct
triumphant but never
disowning its origins, scissors
opening roads in landscapes of cloth,
pilgrim needles zigzagging
through gloss and viridian, crimson,
cotton, a motet of fabric, a lace forest
grown by two hands, one vision.

His theme
over and over:

the twang of plucked
catgut
from which struggles
music,

the tufted swampgrass
quicksilvering
dank meadows,

a baby's resolute fury–metaphysic
of appetite and tension.

Not
the bald image, but always–
undulant, elusive, beyond reach
of any dull
staring eye–lodged

among the words, beneath
the skin of image: nerves,

muscles, rivers
of urgent blood, a mind

secret, disciplined, generous and
unfathomable.
          Over

and over,
his theme
         hid itself and
smilingly reappeared.

                    He loved
persistence–but it must
be linked to invention: landing
backwards, 'facing
into the wind's teeth,'
                    to please him.

He loved
the lotus cup, fragrant
upon the swaying water, loved

the wily mud
pressing swart riches into its roots,

and the long stem of connection.

IV

THE ACOLYTE

Holiday

for K.

i   Postcard

It's not that I can't
get by without you
it's just that
I wasn't lonesome
before I met you.
It's something to do with
salt losing its savor
when that half of the world
one wants to share
stays in one's pocket, half
a crispy delicious bacon sandwich
saved, but for–oh, like Shelley's
posy of dewy flowers, remember,
how he turns to give it–
ah, to whom?

ii   Meeting Again

At Nepenthe, screaming
Steller jays adorn
the gulfs of air. We bask
in sea-sunwarmth. Trees
are blackly green, a phoenix
rages at its prey. I ask
for more coffee and more

231

of your story. You are telling
of suffering, I suffer
hearing it, but rejoice with you
in the jays' blue, their black
heads, the sheen
of feathers and of the sea.
Let's be
best friends: I'll love you
always if you'll love me.

iii   To Eros

Eros, O Eros, hail
thy palate, god who knows
good pasta,
good bread,
good Brie.
　　　　The beauty
of freckled squid, flowers of the sea
fresh off the boat, graces
thy altar, Eros, which is in
our eyes. And on our lips
the blood of berries
before we kiss, before we
stumble to bed.
　　　　Our bed
must be, in thy service, earth—
as the strawberry bed
is earth, a ground
for miracles.
　　　　The flesh
is delicate, we must nourish it:
desire hungers
for wine, for clear plain water,
good strong coffee,
as well as for hard cock and
throbbing clitoris and the
glide and thrust of

sentence and paragraph in and up to the
last sweet sigh of a
chapter's ending.

iv   Love Letter

Fragrant with sandalwood, with lightest
oil of almond,

our hearts still flying around and around
            like silver wheels that
            can't stop spinning
                    all in a moment,

we lay at rest, holding
tight to each other,
                not ready yet
to relax and
each move off into separateness.

Then in words
you gave me
to myself:

you made me know I'd
given you what I
wanted to give,
that I hadn't
been travelling alone . . .
                    You wonder
who you are, if you exist, what
you can do with your energy, has it
a center?
            I tell you,
if you can love a woman
the way you love
blackberries,
strawberries in the sun,

the small red onions you plant,
or a hawk riding
the sway of wind over ocean,
if you can make her know it
even for a moment,

you are as real
as earth itself.
                   No one confirms
an other unless
he himself rays forth
from a center. This
is the human inscape, this
is the design our fragile
shifting molecules strive to utter
upon the airy spaces where it's
so hard to find foothold.

v   **Postcard**

There's a thistle here
smells of meadowsweet–
so sweet,
so meadow-fragrant
among its prickles.
Yarrow is plentiful,
          that China and old England
          both knew had occult
          power–but I can divine
no messages.
              The roses
have no scent. The sea
here is a landlocked Sound.
It says *I miss you,* breaking
quiet upon the dark sand.

She and the Muse

Away he goes, the hour's delightful hero,
arrivederci: and his horse clatters
out of the courtyard, raising
a flurry of straw and scattering hens.

He turns in the saddle waving a plumed hat,
his saddlebags are filled with talismans,
mirrors, parchment histories, gifts and stones,
indecipherable clues to destiny.

He rides off in the dustcloud of his own
story, and when he has vanished she
who had stood firm to wave and watch
from the top step, goes in to the cool

flagstoned kitchen, clears honey and milk and bread
off the table, sweeps from the hearth
ashes of last night's fire, and climbs the stairs
to strip tumbled sheets from her wide bed.

              Now the long-desired
visit is over. The heroine
is a scribe. Returned to solitude,
eagerly she re-enters the third room,

the room hung with tapestries, scenes that change
whenever she looks away. Here is her lectern,
here her writing desk. She picks a quill,
dips it, begins to write. But not of him.

Volupté

Mmm, yes, narcissus, mmm.
Licking my scented fingers.
The squat bulb
complacent under its stars.

The Acolyte

The large kitchen is almost dark.
Across the plain of even, diffused light,
copper pans on the wall and the window geranium
tend separate campfires.
Herbs dangle their Spanish moss from rafters.

At the table, floury hands
kneading dough, feet planted
steady on flagstones,
a woman ponders the loaves-to-be.
Yeast and flour, water and salt,
have met in the huge bowl.

It's not
the baked and cooled and cut
bread she's thinking of,
but the way
the dough rises and has a life of its own,

not the oven she's thinking of
but the way
the sour smell changes
to fragrance.

She wants to put
a silver rose or a bell of diamonds
into each loaf;
she wants

to bake a curse into one loaf,
into another, the words that break
evil spells and release
transformed heroes into their selves;
she wants to make
bread that is more than bread.

V

AGE OF TERROR

The Split Mind

A Governor
is signing papers, arranging deals.
His adored grandchild
sits at his feet; he gives her
the architect's model of the nuclear plant to play with.
'A little house' she says,
'with funny fat chimneys.'
'Goddamn commies,' he mutters, crushing
the report on nuclear hazards into a ball and
tossing it across the room, ignoring
the wastebasket and plutonium and the idea
that he could be wrong, one gesture
sufficing for all.
           He strokes
her shining hair. Her death
is in his hands; in hers
the simulacrum of his will to power,
a funerary playhouse. If he lives
to see her change
in the sick radiance later,
after the plant is built,
what will he tell himself?
How deep, how deep
does the split go, the fault line
under the planned facility,
into his mind?

Engraved

A man and woman
sit by the riverbank.
He fishes,
she reads.
The fish are not biting.
She has not turned the page
for an hour.
The light around them
holds itself taut,
no shadow moves,
but the sky and the woods,
look, are dark.
Night has advanced upon them.

The Vron Woods (North Wales)

In the night's dream of day
the woods were fragrant.
Carapaced, slender, vertical,
            red in the slant
            fragmented light, uprose
Scotch firs,
boughs a vague smoke of
green.
        Underfoot
                    the slipping
of tawny needles.

I was wholly there,
aware of each step
in the hum of quietness,
each breath.
        Sunlight

a net
of discs and lozenges, holding
odor of rosin.

These were the Vron Woods,
felled
seven years before I was born,

levelled,
to feed a war.

Sound of the Axe

Once a woman went into the woods.
The birds were silent. Why? she said.
Thunder, they told her,
thunder's coming.
She walked on, and the trees were dark
and rustled their leaves. Why? she said.
The great storm, they told her,
the great storm is coming.
She came to the river, it rushed by
without reply, she crossed the bridge,
she began to climb
up to the ridge where grey rocks
bleach themselves, waiting
for crack of doom,
and the hermit
had his hut, the wise man
who had lived since time began.
When she came to the hut
there was no one.
But she heard his axe.
She heard
the listening forest.
She dared not follow the sound

240

of the axe. Was it
the world-tree he was felling?
Was this the day?

Desolate Light

We turn to history looking
for vicious certainties through which
voices edged into song,

engorged fringes of anemone swaying
dreamily through deluge,

gray Lazarus bearing
the exquisite itch and ache of blood returning.

Reason has brought us
more dread than ignorance did.
Into the open
well of centuries

we gaze, and see gleaming,
deep in the black broth at the bottom,
chains of hope by which our forebears
hoisted themselves
hand over hand towards light.

But we
stand at the edge looking back in and knowing
too much to reasonably hope. Their desired light
burns us.

O dread,
drought that dries
the ground of joy till it cracks and
caves in,

O dread,
wind that sweeps up the offal of lies,
sweep my knowledge, too, into oblivion,

drop me back in the well.

No avail.

Concurrence

Each day's terror, almost
a form of boredom–madmen
at the wheel and
stepping on the gas and
the brakes no good–
and each day one,
sometimes two, morning-glories,
faultless, blue, blue sometimes
flecked with magenta, each
lit from within with
the first sunlight.

An English Field in the Nuclear Age

To render it!–*this* moment,
                        haze and halos of
                sunbless'd particulars, knowing
no one,
        not lost and dearest nor
        the unfound,
could,
        though summoned,
        though present,
partake nor proffer vision unless

(named, spun, tempered, stain of it
sunk into steel of utterance) it
be wrought:
(centuries furrowed in oakbole, *this* oak,
these dogrose pallors, that very company
of rooks plodding
from stile to stile of the sky):
to render that isolate knowledge, certain
(shadow of oakleaves, larks
urging the green wheat into spires)
there is no sharing save in the furnace,
the transubstantiate, acts
of passion:
(the way

air, *this* minute, searches
warm bare shoulders, blind, a lover,

and how among
thistles, nettles, subtle silver
of long-dried cowpads,

gold mirrors of buttercup satin
assert eternity as they reflect
nothing, everything, absolute instant,
and dread

holds its breath, for
this minute at least was
not the last).

Grey August

The dog's thigh, the absurd heaven,

the dog's thigh extended, thigh of an Odalisque,
the absurdly pale, shrinking, panic of the sky,
an arched heaven of terror,

like an Etruscan outstretched
to partake of wine the dark
relaxed dog, the heavens intimidated
by smog and preparations for thunder, the sensual patient
placing of himself on the cool linoleum
indoors, outdoors the white sky and humid
thick of air, a veiled twilight, his paws
not twitching, his head at rest,

at last something stirs the
ashleaves to sibilance, an ear
flicks up but disregards
this, the dog has not
seen the sky, he will know
thunder when it comes, if it comes
the heavens will retrieve
their pride, the dog's thigh
quivers, it will be,
for this day,
thunder, not war.

Beginners°

Dedicated to the memory of Karen Silkwood anal Eliot Gralla

'*From too much love of living,*
    Hope and desire set free,
Even the weariest river
    Winds somewhere to the sea–'

But we have only begun
to love the earth.

° See note on page 276.

We have only begun
to imagine the fulness of life.

How could we tire of hope?
—so much is in bud.

How can desire fail?
—we have only begun

to imagine justice and mercy,
only begun to envision

how it might be
to live as siblings with beast and flower,
not as oppressors.

Surely our river
cannot already be hastening
into the sea of nonbeing?

Surely it cannot
drag, in the silt,
all that is innocent?
Not yet, not yet—
there is too much broken
that must be mended,

too much hurt we have done to each other
that cannot yet be forgiven.

We have only begun to know
the power that is in us if we would join
our solitudes in the communion of struggle.

So much is unfolding that must
complete its gesture,

so much is in bud.

Psalm: People Power at the Die-in[*]

Over our scattered tents by night
lightning and thunder called to us.

Fierce rain blessed us,
catholic, all-encompassing.

We walked through blazing morning
into the city of law,

of corrupt order, of invested power.

By day and by night
we sat in the dust,

on the cement pavement we sat down and sang.

In the noon of a long day, sharing the work of the play,
we died together, enacting

the death by which all
shall perish unless we act.

•

Solitaries drew close, releasing
each solitude into its blossoming.

We gave to each other the roses
of our communion—

A culture of gardens, horticulture not agribusiness,
arbors among the lettuce, small terrains.

•

[*] See note on page 276.

When we tasted the small, ephemeral
harvest of our striving,

great power flowed from us,
luminous, a promise. Yes! . . .

great energy flowed from solitude,
and great power from communion.

About Political Action in Which
Each Individual Acts from the Heart°

When solitaries draw close, releasing
each solitude into its blossoming,

when we give to each other the roses
of our communion–

a culture of gardens, horticulture not agribusiness,
arbors among the lettuce, small terrains–

when we taste in small victories sometimes
the small, ephemeral yet joyful
harvest of our striving,

great power flows from us,
luminous, a promise. Yes! . . . Then

great energy flows from solitude,
and great power from communion.

° See note on page 276.

Uranium, with which we know
only how to destroy,

lies always under
the most sacred lands–

Australia, Africa, America,
wherever it's found is found an oppressed
ancient people who knew
long before white men found and named it
that there under their feet

under rock, under mountain, deeper
than deepest watersprings, under
the vast deserts familiar
inch by inch to their children

lay a great power.
                    And they knew the folly
of wresting, wrestling, ravaging from the earth
that which it kept
                    so guarded.

Now, now, now at this instant,
men are gouging lumps of that power, that presence,
out of the tortured planet the ancients
say, is our mother.
                    Breaking the doors
of her sanctum, tearing the secret
out of her flesh.

But left to lie, its metaphysical weight
might in a million years have proved
benign, its true force being to be
a clue to righteousness–
showing forth

the human power
not to kill, to choose
not to kill: to transcend
the dull force of our weight and will;

that known profound presence, *un*touched,
the sign
providing witness,
   occasion,
    ritual
for the continuing act of
*non*violence, of passionate
reverence, active love.

In Memory of Muriel Rukeyser

The last event
of Black Emphasis Week.
In the big auditorium, 2 or 3 Whites, 4 or 5 Blacks,
watch the lynching.

In technicolor,
fictive, not
documentary black and white–

the truth, nonetheless,
white and black.

And the burning.
Familiar–
torching of
brittle timber,
or straw.
   Asia or Alabama,
   the screen gives forth
   an odor. Fat. Hair.

There will be bones
in the hot rubble. Black
bones, or yellow,
ash white.

The film continues,
reel after reel. Ends. And now
the few who were here–
                        scattered, like dim lights
of prairie farms seen from a plane,
                          isolate,
                                    lost–
have gone out when you turn to leave.

Out, now, into night.
The world is dark, the movie's over,
it's showing again in your head but
your sobs are silent,
you shake

with despair in the
night which holds

trees, soft air,
music pulsing from a dorm,

and a thousand students who chose
not to attend

the truth of fiction,
history, their own. 'No one

to witness and adjust,'

drifting.
        You think: *Perhaps*

we deserve
no more, we humans,

cruel and dull.
No more time.
                    We've made
our cathedrals,
had our chance,

blown it.

         You will never
feel more alone than this. Or will you?
Yes. There are 'cliffs of fall'
steeper, deeper.

And you remember
the passion for life, the vision
of love and work

your great intelligent friend had,
who died last week.
Is this despair

a link of those chains she called
the sense of shame?

At Scottsboro she
saw plain,
in black and white,

terror
and hatred;

didn't despair,
grieved, worked,
moved beyond shame,

fought forty years more.

You cross
the darkness

still shaking, enter
the house you've been given,

turn up the desk light,
sit down to plan

the next day. How else
to show your respect?

'No one
to drive the car.' *Well,
let's walk then,* she says,
when you imagine her.

Now. Stop shaking. Imagine her.

She was a cathedral.

A Speech: For Antidraft Rally, D.C., March 22, 1980*

As our planet swings and sways
into its new decade
under the raped moon's weary glance,

I've heard the voices
of high-school kids on the bus home to the projects,
of college students (some of them female, this time)
in the swimmingpool locker room, saying,

'If there's a war–' 'If there's a war–'
'I don't want to get drafted but
if there's a war I'll go'–'If there's a war
I'd like to fight' 'If there's a war

* See note on page 276.

I'll get pregnant'
'Bomb Tehran'–'Bomb Moscow' I heard them say.

Ach! They're the same ones, male and female, who ask,
'Which came first, Vietnam or Korea?'
'What was My Lai?' The same kids who think
Ayatollah Khomeini's a, quote, 'Commie.' Who think
World War Two was fought against, quote, 'Reds,' namely
Hitler and some Japs.

No violence they've seen
on the flickering living-room screen familiar since infancy
or the movies of adolescent dates, the dark
so much fuller of themselves, of each other's presence than of
history (and the history anyway
twisted–not that they have a way to know that)–
    the dark
    vibrant with themselves, with warm breath
    half suppressed mirth, the wonder
    of being alive, terrified, entranced
    by sexual fragrance each gives off
    among popcorn, clumsy
    gestures, the weird
    response of laughter when on that screen
    death's happening, 'Wow, *unreal,* and people
    suffer, or dream aloud . . . None of that spoon-fed
       violence
prepares them. The disgusting routine horror of war
eludes them. They think
they would die for something they call America,
vague, as true dreams are not; something they call
freedom, the *Free World,* without ever knowing
what *freedom* means, what *torture* means, what *relative*
       means.
They are free to spray walls with crude
assertions–numbers, pathetic names; free
to disco, to disagree–if they're in school–
with the professor. Great. They don't know
that's not enough, they don't know

ass from elbow, blood from ketchup, that knowledge
is kept from them, they've been taught to assume
if there's a war there's
also a future, they know
not only nothing,
in their criminally neglected imaginations, about
the way war always meant
not only dying but killing,
not only killing but seeing
not only your buddy dying but
your buddy in the act of killing, not nice,
not only
your buddy killing but the dying
of those you
killed yourself, not always
quick, and
not always soldiers.

Yes, not only do draft-age people mostly
not know how that kind of war's become almost a pastoral
compared to *new* war, the kind
in which they may find themselves (while the usual
pinkfaced men, smoothshaved, overfed, placed in power
by the parents of those expendable young, continue
to make the decisions they are programmed for) but also

they know nothing at all about radiation
nothing at all about lasers
nothing at all about how the bombs
the Pentagon sits on like some grotesque
chicken caged in its nest and fed
cancerous hormones, exceed and exceed and exceed
Hiroshima, over and over and over, in weight
                              in power
                              in horror
                              of genocide.
                    When they say
'If there's a war,
I'll go,' they don't know

they would be going to kill
                        themselves,
                        their mamas and papas,
                        brothers and sisters
                        lovers.
When they say, 'If there's a war, I'll get pregnant,'
        they don't seem to know
                        that war would destroy that baby.
When they say, 'I'd like to fight,'
                        for quote, 'freedom,'
                        for quote, the 'Free World,'
                        for quote, 'America,'–
for whatever they think they'd be fighting for,
                those children,
                        those children with braces on their teeth,
                        fears in their notebooks,
                        acne on their cheeks,
                        dreams in their
                                inarticulate hearts
                whom the powerful men at their desks
                designate as the age group suitable for registration,
they don't know they'd be fighting
very briefly, very
successfully,
quite conclusively,
for the destruction of this small
lurching planet, this confused
lump of
rock and soil, ocean and air,
on which our songs, cathedrals, gestures
of faith and splendor
have grown like delicate moss, and now
may or may not survive
the heavy footsteps of our inexcusable ignorance,
the chemical sprays of our rapacious idiocy,
our minds that are big enough
to imagine love, imagine peace, imagine
community–but may not
be big enough to learn in time

how to say no.
                    My dear
fellow-humans, friends, strangers, who would be friends
if there were time–
let us *make* time, let us unite to say
NO to the drift to war, the drift
to take care of little disasters by making a
big disaster and then
the last disaster,
                    from which
no witness will rise,
no seeds.
Let us unite to tell
all we have learned about old-fashioned war's
vomit and shit, about new fashioned war's
abrupt end to all hope–
unite to tell what we know to the wholebodied young,
unwitting victims lined up ready already
like calves at the pen for slaughter;
share what we know, until no more
young voices talk of 'If there's a war,' but all say
No, and again no to the draft, and no to war,
and no to the sacrifice
of anyone's blood to the corporate beast that dreams
it can always somehow
save its own skin.
                    Let our different dream,
and more than dream, our acts
of constructive refusal generate
struggle. And love. We must dare to win
not wars, but a future
in which to live.

For the New Year, 1981

I have a small grain of hope—
one small crystal that gleams
clear colors out of transparency.

I need more.

I break off a fragment
to send you.

Please take
this grain of a grain of hope
so that mine won't shrink.

Please share your fragment
so that yours will grow.

Only so, by division,
will hope increase,

like a clump of irises, which will cease to flower
unless you distribute
the clustered roots, unlikely source—
clumsy and earth-covered—
of grace.

Age of Terror

Between the fear
of the horror of Afterwards
and the despair
in the thought of no Afterwards,
we move abraded,

each gesture scraping us
on the millstones.

In dream
there was an Afterwards:
    the unknown device—
        a silver computer as big as a-
        block of offices at least,
                    floating
        like Magritte's castle on its rock, aloft
        in blue sky–
    did explode,
               there was
    a long moment of cataclysm,
                    light
of a subdued rose-red suffused
all the air before
a rumbling confused darkness ensued,
but
I came to,
      face down,
           and found
my young sister alive near me,
and knew my still younger brother
and our mother and father
                were close by too,
and, passionately relieved, I
comforted my shocked sister,
            still not daring
to raise my head,
only stroking and kissing her arm,
afraid to find devastation around us
though we, all five of us,
seemed to have survived–and I readied myself
to take rollcall: 'Paul Levertoff? Beatrice Levertoff?'

And then in dream–not knowing
if this device, this explosion, were radioactive or not,
but sure that where it had centered

258

there must be wreck, terror,
fire and dust–
the millstones
commenced their grinding again,

and as in daylight
again we were held between them, cramped,
scraped raw by questions:

perhaps, indeed, we were safe; perhaps
no worse was to follow?–but . . .
what of our gladness, when there,
       where the core of the strange
       roselight had flared up
       out of the detonation of brilliant
       angular silver,
there must be others, others in agony,
and as in waking daylight,
the broken dead?

Talk in the Dark

We live in history, says one.
We're flies on the hide of Leviathan, says another.

Either way, says one,
fears and losses.

And among losses, says another,
the special places our own roads were to lead to.

Our deaths, says one.
That's right, says another,
now it's to be a mass death.

Mass graves, says one, are nothing new.

No, says another, but this time there'll be no graves,
all the dead will lie where they fall.

Except, says one, those that burn to ash.
And are blown in the fiery wind, says another.

How can we live in this fear? says one.
From day to day, says another.

I still want to see, says one,
where my own road's going.

I want to live, says another, but where can I live
if the world is gone?

Writing in the Dark

It's not difficult.
Anyway, it's necessary.

Wait till morning, and you'll forget.
And who knows if morning will come.

Fumble for the light, and you'll be
stark awake, but the vision
will be fading, slipping
out of reach.

You must have paper at hand,
a felt-tip pen—ballpoints don't always flow,
pencil points tend to break. There's nothing
shameful in that much prudence: those are your tools.

Never mind about crossing your t's, dotting your i's—
but take care not to cover
one word with the next. Practice will reveal

how one hand instinctively comes to the aid of the other
to keep each line
clear of the next.

Keep writing in the dark:
a record of the night, or
words that pulled you from depths of unknowing,
words that flew through your mind, strange birds
crying their urgency with human voices,

or opened
as flowers of a tree that blooms
only once in a lifetime:

words that may have the power
to make the sun rise again.

Re-Rooting

We were trying to put the roots back,
wild and erratic straying root-limbs,
trying to fit them into the hole that was
cleancut in clay, deep but not
wide enough; or wide but too square—trying
to get the roots back into earth
before they dried out and died.
Ineptly we pulled and pushed
striving to encompass so many rivers
of wood and fiber in one confinement without
snapping the arteries of sap, the force
of life springing in them that made them
spring away from our hands—
we knew our own life was
tied to that strength, that strength we knew would
ebb away if we could not find within us
the blessed guile to tempt

its energy back into earth,
into the quiet depths from which we had
rashly torn it, and now clumsily
struggled to thrust it back not into sinuous corridors
fit for its subtleties, but obstinately
into an excavation dug by machine.
                    And I wake,
as if from dream, but discover
even this digging, better than nothing,
has not yet begun.

Unresolved

'See the blood in the streets'
Neruda

i

Fossil shells, far inland; a god; bones;
they lie exposed by the backhoe.

Little stars continue to confide their silken hopes
among rough leaves.

In blood, his own, a man writes on a wall,
Revolution or Death. Not then. Now.

Now in a dry crevice, the corn, His Grace
the God of Maíz,
wraps his parchment about the green nub
destined to be gold.

ii

When one has begun to believe
the grip of doubt tightens.

A child is born. Earthquake kills
20,000. That's the commonplace.

A dialectic always half perceived. We know
no synthesis.

iii

What we fear begins and begins. Fools and criminals
rule the world. Life is a handful of stones
loosely held in their fists.

iv

Merciful earthquake! Majestic lava pouring
unstinted from mountain's fire! Ceremonious flood!
You ravage but are not hideous. Compare:

chopped-off heads stare in El Salvador
at their steaming torsos, flat circles
                    that were their necks revealing
closepacked flesh and bone and the sectioned tubes
                      through which
food and drink used to pass, and breath. See it on film.

Run the scene over again. And over again.
For verisimilitude, many hundred times
will not be enough.
                      Just out of range—
of the camera, not of the bullets—
babies, tossed high for the Junta's
target practice, plummet
past their parents' upturned screaming faces and hit
the reddening river with small splashes.
Hear it. It sounds like someone idly pitching rocks;
as if a terrified dog were being stoned
while it swam in circles; while it drowned.

v

We know so much of daily bread,
of every thread of lovingly knit compassion;

garments of love clothe us, we rest
our heads upon darkness; when we wake

sapphire transparency calls forth our song.
And this is the very world, the same, the world
of vicious power, of massacre.
Our song is a bird that wants
to sing as it flies, to be
the wings of praise, but doubt

binds tight its wire to hold down
flightbones, choke back breath.
We know no synthesis.

The Great Wave

With my brother I ran
willingly into the sea:

our mother, our sister too,
all of us free and naked.

We knew nothing of risk,
only the sacred pleasure

of sun and sand and the
beckoning ocean:

in, into the leaping
green of the lilt of it.

But at once a vast wave
unfurled itself to seize me, furled

about me, bore me as a bubble
back and tilted aslant from

all shore; all sight, sound, thought of others swept
instantly into

remote distance–
                        Now is wholly
this lucent rampart up which
I can't climb but where
I cling, powerless, unable

to distinguish terror from delight, calm
only in the one wanhope, to keep

a breath alive above the enormous
roar of the sunlaughing utter

force of the great wave, ride
on in its dangerous cradle of swift
transparent silks that curve
in steel over and round me, bearing

westward, outward, beyond
all shores, the great

wave still mounting, moving,
poised and poised in its

flood of emerald, dark unshatterable
crystal of its

unfathomed purpose–

Mass for the Day of St. Thomas Didymus

i   Kyrie

O deep unknown, guttering candle,
beloved nugget lodged
in the obscure heart's
last recess,
have mercy upon us.

We choose from the past, tearing morsels to feed
pride or grievance.
We live in terror
of what we know:

death, death, and the world's
death we imagine
       and cannot imagine,
we who may be
the first and the last witness.

We live in terror
of what we do not know,
in terror of not knowing,
of the limitless, through which freefalling
forever, our dread
sinks and sinks,
          or
       of the violent closure of all.

Yet our hope lies
in the unknown,
in our unknowing.

O deep, remote unknown,
O deep unknown,
Have mercy upon us.

ii   Gloria

Praise the wet snow
       falling early.
Praise the shadow
       my neighbor's chimney casts on the tile roof
even this gray October day that should, they say,
have been golden.
              Praise
the invisible sun burning beyond
    the white cold sky, giving us
light and the chimney's shadow.
Praise
god or the gods, the unknown,
that which imagined us, which stays
our hand,
our murderous hand,
               and gives us
still,
in the shadow of death,
      our daily life,
      and the dream still
of goodwill, of peace on earth.
Praise
flow and change, night and
the pulse of day.

iii   Credo

I believe the earth
exists, and
in each minim mote
of its dust the holy
glow of thy candle.
Thou
unknown I know,
thou spirit,
giver,
lover of making, of the
wrought letter,
wrought flower,
iron, deed, dream.
Dust of the earth,
help thou my
unbelief. Drift,
gray become gold, in the beam of
vision. I believe and
interrupt my belief with
doubt. I doubt and
interrupt my doubt with belief. Be,
belovéd, threatened world.
             Each minim
mote.
      Not the poisonous
luminescence forced
out of its privacy,
the sacred lock of its cell
broken. No,
the ordinary glow
of common dust in ancient sunlight.
Be, that I may believe. Amen.

iv   Sanctus

Powers and principalities–all the gods,
angels and demigods, eloquent animals, oracles,
storms of blessing and wrath–

> all that Imagination
> has wrought, has rendered,
> striving, in throes of epiphany–
>
> naming, forming–to give
> to the Vast Loneliness
> a hearth, a locus–

send forth their song towards
the harboring silence, uttering
the ecstasy of their names, the multiform
name of the Other, the known
Unknown, unknowable:

sanctus, hosanna, sanctus.

v   Benedictus

Blesséd is that which comes in the name of the spirit,
that which bears
the spirit within it.

The name of the spirit is written
in woodgrain, windripple, crystal,

in crystals of snow, in petal, leaf,
moss and moon, fossil and feather,

blood, bone, song, silence,
very word of
very word,

flesh and
vision.

      (But what of the deft infliction
      upon the earth, upon the innocent,
      of hell by human hands?

      Is the word
      audible under or over the gross
      cacophony of malevolence?
      Yet to be felt
            on the palm, in the breast,
      by deafmute dreamers,
            a vibration
            known in the fibers of
            the tree of nerves, or witnessed
            by the third eye to which
            sight and sound are one?

      What of the emptiness,
      the destructive vortex that whirls
      no word with it?)

In the lion's indolence,
    there spirit is,
in the tiger's fierceness
    that does not provide in advance
but springs
        only as hunger prompts,
        and the hunger
        of its young.

Blesséd is that which utters
its being,
the stone of stone,
the straw of straw,
            for there
spirit is.
      But can the name

utter itself
in the downspin of time?
Can it enter
the void?
Bléssed
be the dust. From dust the world
utters itself. We have no other
hope, no knowledge.
The word
chose to become
flesh. In the blur of flesh
we bow, baffled.

vi   Agnus Dei

Given that lambs
are infant sheep, that sheep
are afraid and foolish, and lack
the means of self-protection, having
neither rage nor claws,
venom nor cunning,
what then
is this 'Lamb of God'?

This pretty creature, vigorous
to nuzzle at milky dugs,
woolbearer, bleater,
leaper in air for delight of being, who finds in astonishment
four legs to land on, the grass
all it knows of the world?
With whom we would like to play,
whom we'd lead with ribbons, but may not bring
into our houses because
it would soil the floor with its droppings?

What terror lies concealed
in strangest words, *O lamb*
of God that taketh away

the Sins of the World: an innocence
                    smelling of ignorance,
                    born in bloody snowdrifts,
                    licked by forebearing
dogs more intelligent than its entire flock put together?

                              God then,
                    encompassing all things, is
                    defenseless? Omnipotence
                    has been tossed away, reduced
                    to a wisp of damp wool?

                              And we,
                    frightened, bored, wanting
only to sleep till catastrophe
has raged, clashed, seethed and gone by without us,
                              wanting then
to awaken in quietude without remembrance of agony,

                    we who in shamefaced private hope
                    had looked to be plucked from fire and given
                    a bliss we deserved for having imagined it,

                              is it implied that *we*
                    must protect this perversely weak
                    animal, whose muzzle's nudgings
                    suppose there is milk to be found in us?
                    Must hold to our icy hearts
                    a shivering God?

                              •

So be it.
            Come, rag of pungent
            quiverings,
                    dim star.
                              Let's try
                    if something human still

can shield you,
                    spark
of remote light.

The Many Mansions

What I must not forget
is the world of the white herons

complete to the last hair of pondweed,
a world the size of an apple,

perfect and undefiled, with its own sky, its air,
flora and fauna, distance, mysteries.

What I must not forget
is the knowledge that vision gave me

that it was not a fragile, only, other world,
there were, there are (I learned) a host,

each unique, yet each having
the grace of recapitulating

a single radiance, multiform.

This is what, remembering,
I must try, telling myself again,

to tell you. For that the vision
was given me: to know and share,

        passing from hand to hand, although
        its clarity dwindles in our confusion,

the amulet of mercy.

Notes

85   'Chekhov on the West Heath.' The West Heath is a section of Hampstead Heath, the tract of never-cultivated land that overlooks London from the north and includes the point of highest elevation in the London area.

86   'The small, dark-green volumes. / The awkward, heroic versions' refers to the English collected edition of Constance Garnett's pioneer translations.

Für Elise is a short piano piece by Beethoven.

87   'The Black Monk' is a Chekhov story often, or perhaps I should say usually, interpreted quite differently–that is, as being a sad story about illusion. I did not then, and do not now, see it that way. All the *apparent* illusion in it is in fact what is strong and positive!

'The betrothed girl' is the heroine of the story variously translated as 'The Betrothed,' 'A Marriageable Girl,' 'The Bride,' etc.

89   'tender, delightful, ironic'–from Gorki's reminiscences of Chekhov. However, just about everyone who ever described Chekhov mentioned his smile in very similar terms.

122   shadowgraph–this is factual and may be viewed at Hiroshima.

131   'The Phonecall.' Debs–Eugene V. Debs, who declared in a speech in court on September 11, 1918: '. . . while there is a lower class, I am in it; while there is a criminal element, I am of it; while there is a soul in prison, I am not free.'

136   'Dream: Château de Galais' refers to Alain Fournier's *Le Grand Meaulnes (The Wanderer).*

140   'Modulations': 'the divine animal/who carries us through the world.' Ralph Waldo Emerson, *The Poet:* '. . . beyond the energy of [the] possessed and conscious intellect [one] is capable of a new energy (as of an intellect doubled on itself,) by abandonment to the nature of things. . . . As a traveller who has lost his way throws his reins on his horse's neck and trusts to the instinct of the animal to find his road, so must we do with the divine animal who carries us through this world.'

158 'Blake's Baptismal Font'–the font, in St. James's, Piccadilly, is one of Grinling Gibbons's few works in marble.

192 'The Dragon-Fly Mother.' Readers may be interested to read 'The Earthwoman and the Waterwoman' (*Collected Earlier Poems,* p. 31), a poem written in 1957, to which this 1979 poem makes some allusions.

220. 'Winter Afternoons in the V. & A., pre-W. W. II' For those unfamiliar with London: the V. & A. is the Victoria and Albert Museum in South Kensington. Nowadays it is crowded with visitors.

244 'Beginners.' The opening stanza is Swinburne, slightly misquoted because I had remembered it this way for many years.

246 'Psalm: People Power . . .' and 'About Political Action . . .' The long
247 version derives directly from events described in prose as 'With the Seabrook Natural Guard in Washington, 1978' (*Light Up the Cave,* p. 162). The short version, detached from that particular occasion, is an alternative rather than a substitute.

252 'A Speech . . .' Written for an antidraft rally (which was attended by 35,000) this piece really *is* a speech, and not properly classifiable as a poem. I decided to include it because it is not prose either, and because many people–draft counsellors and high-school teachers especially–have requested me to make it generally available.

INDEX OF TITLES